A Woman's Life
in Service of the Eternal

A Woman's Life in Service of the Eternal

*My Path as the
Teaching Prophetess and Emissary of God
at this Turn of Time*

Gabriele

A Woman's Life in Service of the Eternal
My Path as the Teaching Prophetess and Emissary of God
at This Turn of Time – Gabriele
First Edition, May 2017
Published by:
© Gabriele-Verlag Das Wort GmbH
Max-Braun-Str. 2 – 97828 Marktheidenfeld – Germany
www.gabriele-verlag.com
www.gabriele-publishing-house.com

Original German title:
Ein Frauenleben im Dienste des Ewigen
Mein Weg als Lehrprophetin und Botschafterin Gottes
in dieser Zeitenwende – Gabriele

The German edition is the work of reference for all
questions regarding the meaning of the contents
Authorized translation from
Gabriele-Verlag Das Wort GmbH

All rights reserved.

Printed by: KlarDruck GmbH, Marktheidenfeld, Germany

Order No. S 551en
ISBN: 978-3-89201-814-8

Table of Contents

About the Eternal Word 11

Foreword from 2016 13

Foreword from the Year 1997 21

A Woman's Life in Service of the Eternal
**My Path as the Teaching Prophetess and Emissary
of God at this Turn of Time – Gabriele** 25

A Word to the Reader (1997) 27

Key Thoughts to Think About 29

1. My Life from Childhood
   Until Relocation to Würzburg 35

   Childhood 35

   Child, Say "Grüß Gott!" 41

   *Sense of Justice, Dynamism and Bubbling
   Vitality – the Expression of an Alert,
   Powerful Soul* 44

   *For Church Christians, God Is Far Away.
   "Sadly, God Cannot Hear Me ..."* 47

   First Years of Marriage and Relocation to Würzburg 52

2. My Life in Würzburg Until the Breakthrough of the Inner Word 57

A New Rhythm of Life in the Quiet House in Würzburg 57

The Far-reaching Shock: The Surprising Death of My Mother. Does Life Go On? 59

Questions After Questions About the Contextual Meaning of Life and About God 63

The Turn to the Spiritual. An Inner Process of Realization 66

Inwardness Through Prayer. Nature, the Teacher 69

The Inner Experience: Life Continues After the Earthly Existence. There Is a God of Love 71

Knowledge About the Meaning of Life on Earth. The Soul's Spiritual Potential Urges Toward the Light 75

During Prayer Meetings, More Impulses for My Inner Life. The Certainty: God Lives in Me! The Person Becomes Aware of the Soul's Knowledge 77

A Growing Nearness to God 80

Harbingers of the Prophetic Word 82

3. My Path as the Teaching Prophetess and
   Emissary of God Until the Year 1997 87

*Breakthrough of the Prophetic Word.
First Lesson From Christ and From
the Divine-Spiritual Teacher Brother Emanuel* 87

The Voice of God Through the Prophets 92

*My Spiritual Teacher: Brother Emanuel,
the Cherub of Divine Wisdom* 95

*The Great Task: A Worldwide Work.
Notification of Attacks, Defamations
and Persecution of Christians* 101

*The Rapid Growth of the Divine Work.
Steadfastness and Strength for the Life
and Work in the Spirit of God* 106

*Further and Deeper Training by My Spiritual Teacher,
Brother Emanuel.
The Step-by-Step Guidance Toward the
Absolute Consciousness* 108

*To Be a Prophet Is the Call and the Calling by God.
Soul and Person – A Prisoner in Service of God* 113

*To Live in the World, but Not With the World.
The Teaching Prophetess and Emissary of God* 116

*A Proponent of the Eternal Truth,
of the Law of Life, Is Not Always Comfortable
for His Fellow People* 121

*The Church Institution Broke into Our Family Life
with Intrigues and Defamations* 124

Lonely Among People 126

*From Early in the Morning Until Late –
I Am Always There, Responsibly* 128

For the Reader 130

The Workings of Gabriele, the Divine Wisdom – Sophia – in the Earthly Garment 131

*Gabriele, the Emissary of God, Travelled to
Many Countries of the Earth on Behalf of the Eternal* 135

The Beginning of New Jerusalem 139

The Illusion "I Know Her" – Contemporary Witnesses Report 147

A Contemporary Witness 152

    Her Life in a Foreign Land 157

    Great Moments 159

    Dialogue with God 161

    How Manuscripts Develop 164

    The Designer 166

    Gabriele's Nature 171

    The Divine Wisdom, Sophia, Who Prepares the Way for the Christ of God 172

Another Contemporary Witness 175

Gabriele, the Exalted Woman, the Lily of God, Sophia 185

Suggested Reading 205

About the Eternal Word

You Wisdom's truest nature,
the image of the Father's heart!
you articulate All
and eternally vivid life,
by whom the power of becoming
was given to the entire world!

The essence of all creatures emblazoned on your shield.
In you the mild wealth of grace revealed.
Salvation resolved hovers over you since eternity,
which you, Primordial-All-Knowingness are wont to raise
and free the poor quarry from the hunter's net.

Self-reliant and true word, most secret angel's wonder,
you unutterable God, but yet believed in hearts,
you Seraph's honor, do you step down so low?

You increase your honor all the more,
by turning away our need.
Give me, O source of words, o lofty wise one to laud you.
Yea, speak and express yourself,
what I could not extoll enough!

(Catharina Regina von Greiffenberg, 1633-1694)

Foreword from 2016

During this time, we are witnesses of a unique event in the known history of humankind. The Kingdom of God reveals itself through His prophetess and emissary, Gabriele, and leads us into the whole truth, insofar as it can be conveyed with human words.

Never before was it possible for the message from the Kingdom of God, conveyed through a prophet or prophetess of God, to be directly and authentically recorded and made available worldwide in unadulterated form to all people in the present and future times.

Just as unique is the fact that the prophet herself speaks about her life and work from her opened divine consciousness, and that this treasure is preserved, complete and unadulterated, for all people in the present and future time.

How particularly invaluable the knowledge of the life and work of a divine being among human beings is can be easily recognized by the example of the greatest prophet, the Christ of God, the Redeemer of all souls and ensouled people, who lived among the people as Jesus of Nazareth. His whole life and work was a single symbol for humankind. That is why His whole life and work are part of the message from the Kingdom of God to humankind.

It is no different with all the great prophets of God, from Abraham, to Elijah, Moses, Isaiah, Jeremiah and many others. And it especially applies to Gabriele, who for over 40 years has been working among us as the representative of the Kingdom of God in service of the Eternal One.

That in this book, Gabriele writes about herself, about her life and works is, however, anything but a matter of course, for it is not at all part of her nature.

A true prophet of God is solely a representative and speaking instrument of the Kingdom of God on Earth. The will of the Eternal and the prophet's calling through Him is the prophet's purpose in life; all the prophet's thoughts and energies are devoted to the mission from the Kingdom of God. Nor is it the prophet who calls himself a prophet – the prophet bows before the will of the Eternal when He expresses this through the prophet.

This is also true of Gabriele. It goes against her nature to bring her person, herself, into prominence in any way. At every moment, she is distinguished by her particular reticence and modesty. She gives the honor solely to God, the Eternal, for everything that she accomplishes through her incomparable talents and abilities.

When Gabriele said that even so, she was willing to report about her own life, this was done solely under the motivation to support and help others with what she had gone through and experienced. Under this condition, these autobiographical memoirs also came about, which Gabriele wrote down in 1997, about 22 years after her calling by the eternal All-One to be the prophetess and emissary of God.

In the manuscript entitled: *"A Woman's Life in Service of the Eternal. My Path as the Teaching Prophetess and Emissary of God at this Turn of Time,"* Gabriele describes her life's path from early youth until 1997 as God's teaching prophetess and emissary. It is another gem from what she herself has written, which, authentic and unadulterated, can serve this and future generations as help and guidance.

And yet, external circumstances prevented the book from being published back then.

In 1997, when Gabriele had finished the manuscript, the already ongoing 20-year campaign of the church Inquisition against the word of the Christ of God and His prophetess and emissary, Gabriele, was approaching a new high point. At that time, the character assassination instigated by the institutional mainstream churches, which Gabriele also mentions in her manuscript, was assuming ever worse forms. With every opportunity that presented itself, droves of so-called church experts poured the basest filth of denominational origin over the word of the Eternal and His prophetess, Gabriele. Via the press, radio and television, dependent and unscrupulous representatives of the media spread the wickedest untruths according to the allegations of the pulpit-preachers.

The defamations and discriminations compounded into character assassination; they didn't dare go any further. However, the protagonist of the church character assassinators, a Protestant-Lutheran pastor, made no secret of his mindset. He publicly stated: "When you bet on the Inquisition with me, of course, you are correct," and in another place, he called to one of his victims: "In the Middle Ages, we would have dealt with you entirely differently."

Back then, in the same demonic spirit, a Catholic mayor also waged a campaign of character assassination and ostracism against his fellow citizens who professed to the work of the Christ of God

These are only two examples of many incidents that were the order of the day back then. In this poisoned environment, it was decided not to publish Gabriele's autobiography, so that people, as always, would not have to again suffer for the sake of truth. This decision was also made so as not to supply the Inquisition with any further excuse to renew their accusations against the sublime word from the Kingdom of God and against His prophetess, Gabriele.

And so, at that time, the manuscript remained unpublished.

Meanwhile, 20 years have gone by. Much has changed since then.

Undeterred, despite all adversities and attacks, Gabriele continued her activities in service of the Eternal for the work of the Christ of God. Through Gabriele's tireless dedication and input, the worldwide work, about which Christ had spoken to her over and over again at the beginning of her prophetic development, has taken shape. During this time, God, the Eternal, His Son Christ, the Co-Regent of the heavens, and the Cherub of divine Wisdom gave revelations through Gabriele.

Through Gabriele, thousands of pages emerged in countless books, writings and schoolings. Hundreds of radio and television programs were produced. The word from the Kingdom of God, conveyed through Gabriele, goes out around the whole globe via approximately one thousand radio and television stations. The work of the Christ of God radiates into the whole world. The atmosphere of the Christ of God is building up all around the Earth. And externally, the foundations for the Kingdom of Peace are visible – the onset of New Jerusalem.

At the same time, what was foretold to Gabriele from the Kingdom of God already at the beginning of her prophetic office has come to pass. The cassock-wearers, the violators of the laws of God, exposed themselves through their defamations, mockeries and malicious gossip. Everything they used to malign the character of others was exposed as their own fluidum, their aura. Their power is diminishing. Their true nature is becoming ever more visible – as well as whom they serve and belong with. The inspirer of the cassock-wearers, whom the Christ of God in Jesus of Nazareth described as the father of lies, the father from below, has been cast onto the Earth from the spheres of the beyond. He is raging and rearing up one last time. It is the last act of his demonic doings.

During this time, God, the Eternal, again spoke mightily to His children, on August 14, 2016. To all ensouled human beings and to all souls, He revealed who it is that lives among them as prophetess and emissary of God under the earthly name of Gabriele.

God, the Eternal, said the following:

I, who I Am, present the lily to My daughter from My primordial heart, who has assumed the prophetic word for Me and is the emissary of the eternal kingdom.

As a human being, she is the expression of Sophia, the Wisdom, to whom I present the lily. My word, the truth, spoke, and speaks through her. My word of purity is the prophetic word and the voice of Wisdom.

I Am who I Am, from the primordial beginning. She is who she is, from Me, from the primordial beginning. Before the act of creation, she was in Me as My ideal image and will, and I created her as My image.

I sent My image, the primordial Wisdom, the divine Wisdom, to the human beings. She became a human being, was a human being and is still a human being among the human beings, My primordially eternal ideal image.

I was the word through her. I Am the word through her. In her soul, I Am the primordial Being, the lily, which she places into the hearts of all people who walk the path of purity and love, the messianic path in the sophianic age.

With this mighty revelation, God, the Eternal, ushered in a new age worldwide, the messianic and sophianic age. It is the path of the Christ of God for people in the new era who strive for a higher culture and a peaceful communality.

What the words of the Eternal truly mean is certainly not at all comprehensible to the human consciousness, nor what a deep connection has existed between God, the Most High, and Sophia, the divine Wisdom, since the very beginning of the Being, before the event of creation began. This being from the heavens, the Seraph of the princely pair of the divine Wisdom, the Sophia, to whom the Eternal presents the lily as a symbol of purity and love, lives among us as the human being Gabriele. And in the messianic and sophianic age, her work, the workings of Sophia, along with the messianic workings of the Christ of God, is a mainstay of the work of guiding all fallen beings back home.

After this mighty divine revelation and further explanations from the Kingdom of God, more attention was directed to the entire life on Earth and the works of Sophia in Gabriele, the prophetess and emissary of God. With more detailed research into earlier divine revelations, many an indication has been found on the true nature, on the true origin of Gabriele as Sophia, as has now been so mightily revealed by God, the Eternal. While looking into earlier documents from Gabriele's life, we again became aware of the autobiographical writings of Gabriele, *"A Woman's Life in Service of the Eternal. My Path as the Teaching Prophetess and Emissary of God at this Turn of Time."*

We are particularly glad that we can now make this gem, this manuscript, available to you as a book. It has lost none of its timeless relevance. And its content is just as touching, partly distressing, but also as deeply impressive as back then.

While reading, we ask that you bear in mind that the manuscript was written in 1997, and that time-related information referring to the year 1997 is given as if in the present. In this respect, nothing was changed in the manuscript.

Foreword
From the Year 1997

An autobiography is always related to the person. Anyone who knows our sister Gabriele, the teaching prophetess and emissary of God in our time, knows that there is hardly any human being who is less likely to show herself, to spread around personal aspects about herself and to make a lot of words about her thinking and living. Gabriele's life is – in a high spiritual sense – not a personal, but a totally impersonal life, which is not focused on itself, the person. She does not live in this world for herself, but in service of the Eternal for her fellow people, for nature and the animals, for all of creation. That is impersonal life. Since about 1975, her life has been a daily devotion to God in selfless service for her brothers and sisters.

Why does a person who is in the Spirit of God, that is, a person who lives impersonally, write an autobiography? The answer: Because that person is impersonal and does not want to gain anything for himself with it. We received the following answer to this question directed to our sister Gabriele: "Why are you now writing an autobiography?":

If it were solely about me, it would certainly not have come to this book. I am not important.

The prophetic event has to be seen in a larger context.

At every great turn of time, God has sent prophets. About the prophets of the Old Covenant – and also about the prophets of the time after Jesus – few authentic records have been passed down that provide information about the nature of the prophetic word, about the development to becoming a prophet and about the inner processes that are connected with the prophetic office. That is why I have frequently been asked during the past years to write down my experiences and publish them in book form. Because this is, above all, the will of God, whom I may serve, with this, I pass on several records to the public. They are merely a few descriptions in comparison to what I had to learn, experience and suffer.

The Lord wants the present generation and future generations to learn about what greatness is taking place, or took place, in this time through Him, the Eternal.

This time is a mighty turn of time, because life on this Earth will change radically, and that, to an extent that no inhabitant of the Earth can imagine today. In the manifold signs of the time, many recognize the evidence indicating the so-called final battle between light and darkness. The world of egocentricity and materialism is gradually fading away.

The age of the Spirit of Christ, as He taught His apostles and disciples, is rising and shaping the new era.

To bear lawful fruit on the Earth, the Kingdom of God, the Kingdom of Peace, which Jesus, the Christ, taught, has to grow out of each person's soul. Time is like a ripe fruit.

People who live a God-filled life, who keep the laws of God, make peace with their fellowman. Only then will there be peace on this Earth, and the Kingdom of Peace can be raised.

Followers of Jesus of Nazareth view it this way: The life of our sister Gabriele is not only the life of an extraordinary human being. It is a testimony, a shining example of God's wisdom and greatness, and of His mighty workings, particularly during this time.

We are glad that Gabriele made the decision to tell about her life. Much of what she reports and presents is generally valid and can serve as example and orientation for a person striving toward God. As a woman and as a sister, as a person who lives in the Spirit of God, she is a guide for all people seeking God. We thank our eternal Father that she is with us.

Followers of Jesus of Nazareth

A Woman's Life in Service of the Eternal

My Path as the Teaching Prophetess and Emissary of God at this Turn of Time

Gabriele

A Word to the Reader (1997)

This book contains substantial parts of my autobiography. In addition to the publications of past years, in these statements I am giving further insight into my thinking and living. Here, I also describe, in a general way, my surroundings and life with the people who were and are around me daily, as well as those who caused me many torments of hell.

When I leave this world, I will remain in the memory of many people as the prophetess and emissary of God. During my whole time as the instrument of the Eternal, I have never placed importance on having my fellow people call me prophetess or emissary of God. This is how God, the Eternal, spoke, and speaks, of me, His servant. I myself feel as a sister of my brothers and sisters. This is how I have lived and this is also how I want to remain – as a sister in the hearts of my brothers and sisters and in the hearts of all people who have heard, and hear, about me.

God is the heaven, the love and the light. From this infinite, eternal consciousness of love, of the Being, I greet my brothers and sisters.

Gabriele

Key Thoughts to Think About

Is God really silent? – The reactions to this question vary. Some people feel provoked; others shrug their shoulders. Still others think about it and others simply retort: "I believe in God!"

A clear statement, one would think. The one who formulates it often thinks that with this he has said everything, that he has made a profession which leaves nothing to doubt. But let's take a closer look. What is the "belief" or "faith" that so many talk about? Is "belief" merely a word, or is the activity of the belief at work in it, the actualization of what Jesus, the Christ of God, taught us and lived as an example for us?

Many say: "Well, a person simply believes in God and Christ because that's how he learned it at home and in school." But does the living faith that changes our life lie in these words? Many pray to the Eternal. But is the content of the prayer a living reality in the daily life of the one praying, or is it merely a prescribed prayer from a prayer book?

Still others say: "Well, God spoke through prophets in the Old Covenant, but that was a long time ago." Many are definitely of the opinion that Jesus of Nazareth, the Son of the eternal Father who became a human being, was the greatest prophet of all time. But what effect does this have in their life?

The faith of most people is thus a passive faith and not the active faith, the Christianity of the deed.

For many, God is somewhere in a place far from human beings, or in the tabernacle and in the monstrance of church institutions. The mainstream churches have shaped this viewpoint, because they have forbidden the great Spirit, God, to speak in their ranks – through the doctrine that God no longer speaks to the people through the mouth of a prophet since Jesus of Nazareth. This doctrine essentially says that God spoke in the Old Covenant and that the theologians speak in the New Covenant. Note well: This is a doctrine, which God, the Eternal, does not follow. He does not have any opinions – He knows.

Jesus said: *I have yet many things to say to you, but you cannot bear them now. When the Spirit of truth comes, he will guide you into all the truth.*

If the theologians would not only talk about their Bible, but live according to the truth, which the Bible also still contains – despite the many encroaching influences – then they would have to give up these doctrines and be brothers among brothers and sisters.

The Catholic Church thinks that it is the only Church that can grant salvation. Until the present time (1997), the Comforter, the Holy Spirit, has not guided the church believers into all the truth. The church institutions, also the "only saving Church," are set in their traditions. And so, they have driven away the living Spirit. And because this rigidity is a centuries-old tradition, they also drive thinking people out of their theological thinking apparatus, which they teach as their truth.

If theologians would teach what Jesus taught the people and lived as an example for them, among other things, that each person is the temple of God, and if they would teach that all honor should be given solely to the One who dwells in the temple of flesh and bone, and that God is able to speak to all those people who resolve for the order of the temple in themselves, then they would have to admit that theologians are superfluous. That would be too much for those who like to hear themselves talk. They would then no longer be the ones who receive honor, but like all people, listeners of the holy word, which is to be actualized in life for the honor of God.

God, our eternal Father, does not comply with theological opinions, nor according to human interpretations of the Bible, nor with the opinions of Saul, who much later became Paul. He, the great All-One, loves His children and will also reveal Himself to His children through the mouth of a prophet and talk to them – just as any loving father does. He, the great Spirit, does not allow His children to become orphans, particularly in this mighty turn of time in which humankind finds itself – a time in which the old structures no longer apply, when ever more is collapsing and everyone is against everyone.

Many Bible believers say: "But we have the Bible and thus, the word of God." But if you think about the fact that the Bible contains only copies of copies, into which much was edited and many things changed, you have to wonder: Who knows what the word of God is? Anyone who does not fulfill the Ten Commandments of God, which Moses brought us, and does not live the principles of the law in the Sermon on the Mount, which Jesus, the Christ, taught and lived as an example for us, lacks the ability to discern between God's word and the work of man. Even if we were to assume that falsifications were not deliberately made, the question arises: Did the authors of the copies of copies fulfill the Ten Commandments and the Sermon on the Mount, so that they were filled with God's wisdom – or did they edit their own ideas into the texts?

If we want to infer the truth from the Bible, then we first have to fulfill the Ten Commandments and the Sermon on the Mount. Then our consciousness will expand and we will attain the ability to discern. This comes from the law of God.

So anyone who does not fulfill the Ten Commandments of God and the Sermon on the Mount will not find the truth in the Bible, and will allow himself to be deluded by the ideas and opinions that were worked into the texts.

Every person is responsible for his own thinking, speaking and doing. The responsibility remains with him, even when he thinks he can base himself on other people, on theologians, for instance, and when he makes himself dependent on copies of copies of copies. The Ten Commandments are known to every person and many also know the Sermon on the Mount, which ends with the words: *The one who hears these words of Mine and does them ...* Anyone can measure his way of thinking and living against these words. They are also the criterion for all other biblical texts.

God, our Father, the infinite, all-permeating love, lets no child out of His great Father-heart. However, there are many people who can no longer believe in this unending love of the Father. For them, the heavenly Father is far away. It is difficult to imagine Him and perhaps He is even feared. That He is very close to us and wants the best for each of us, that we can trust Him – all that is no longer comprehensible to many people.

Why is it that many can no longer believe in the kind, all-loving Father? Isn't it primarily because a dogmatic, tradition-bound, rigid theology has distorted the image of God, our Father, thus leading to an alienation of the person from God?

We know that the Spirit of God was alive in early Christianity. He blew in the first Christian communities and taught and guided the followers of Jesus of Nazareth by way of the prophetic word. The Apocalypse of John also bears witness to the prophetic spirit after the life of Jesus on Earth. One can forbid God to speak in the mainstream churches and churches of power, but He, the great Spirit, knows the way to renew the call to His children again and again, to teach them and to guide them into more profound truths, which Jesus Himself announced to us.

The Christ of God will not be silenced. He has always sent prophets who brought His love and wisdom to the Earth, in order to guide the people, His children, on the path to the heart of love. Many prophets and prophetesses, bringers of truth, were hushed up or silenced by the churches of power.

But the Spirit of God blows where He will, and now is the time in which what was foretold is being fulfilled.

1.
My Life From Childhood Until Relocation to Würzburg

Childhood

I was born in southern Germany in 1933. My parents were simple craftspeople who worked day after day for the livelihood of their family. My father was a master tailor and my mother was a seamstress by profession. Their marriage produced two children.

We owned a house with a garden and my father's tailor shop was also in the house. During the first years of marriage, my mother still worked as a seamstress. After my birth, she became primarily housewife and mother. My grandmother also lived in our family. When my brother was born over a decade after the end of the war, our family then consisted of 5 members: father, mother, grandmother and the two children.

There was nothing special about our family. We were an average family like countless others. We were all brought up in the Catholic faith, because each of us was baptized into it as an infant, without heeding what Jesus had taught: Teach first, then baptize. We attended Mass every Sunday, as

Catholicism prescribes. There is not much to report about my parents' home. My parents had friends, just as many families have friends. They loved socializing, just as many families love to socialize. The family had many relatives and we visited each other. So there was nothing special to say about it.

I had a close child-parent relationship with my father as well as my mother. My father was very concerned about providing for the family. He was called up for military duty at the beginning of World War II.

With the work of their hands, my mother and grandmother endeavored to acquire the necessities of life and to maintain house and garden. Mother's serious, yet sunny disposition frequently contributed to brightening things up, even during the hard time of war. I inherited much of her earnestness paired with cheerfulness. Our similar predispositions and fear for the life of my father, who was a soldier, provided much common ground, so that as child, youth and as an adult, I frequently went to my mother, who was understanding in many situations and, through her character, helped me to become a sincere and just person.

I started school during the war. So I was a school child of the war. This meant that in our daily life and at school many things did not run as in normal times. There were also a few deficiencies in the school system, for instance, the lack of teachers. Because younger men had been drafted for military duty, we were taught primarily by older teachers. During the last years of the war, classes were cancelled ever more frequently because of air-raid warnings. That was totally alright with us children – but we didn't learn much this way – actually, only what was really needed for life, like reading, writing, arithmetic and a little local history.

During this time, we children often had to go along to "forage," so to speak. I was seven or eight years old when my mother took me along to the villages to ask for eggs, milk and bread. We often walked for hours from farm to farm for a few eggs or pieces of bread. Now and then a little bartering was done. Shoes or shoe soles would be bartered for butter, eggs and bread.

A new dress was sewn from two old dresses or an old garment was turned and a "new one" made from it. Worn-out sweaters were unraveled to knit a scarf, for instance, or to use the wool to mend socks or to mix several colors of wool and knit a new sweater from them. Through this, many a one learned to save and to work carefully with what he had. Every used carton, every sheet of paper, every piece of string and every button was put aside – nothing was thrown away. It could perhaps be used for something.

During that time, people drew closer together. Through external adversity, through the chaos of war, they were more dependent on one another than in the good days. One helped the other, because we had learned that when today we were still able to help others – tomorrow we might need the help ourselves.

The effects of war could be felt all over Germany. Cities were bombed; many houses in towns and villages were damaged; hunger and hardship was everywhere. The economy collapsed, bartering flourished. Many of life's essentials were not available even when you had food ration coupons for them.

The war years had marked my father. To a certain extent, he was very closed, because he had experienced a lot during this time. He had not only seen wounded and dying soldiers, but he himself had lain wounded in Dresden and barely escaped the destruction and bombing of this city. When at the end of the war, he fled through the woods and returned to his home village and to his own home, he saw many soldiers hung for "desertion," and for years he had a hard time forgetting them.

We children heard and experienced all this during the years of war and after it. Hardship and privation taught us to be frugal. The prayer of thanks at the table was not merely a cliché for us, because I had seen that in the morning mother did not yet know what she would put on the table at noontime. There was little to snack on.

Simplicity and thrift, practiced from childhood, have helped me my life long to get by with little in the way of material goods. So even today, it is still easy for me to sew a dress from remnants, for instance, or, with little effort, to turn a room full of nooks and crannies into a comfortable living room, and as before, it is a matter of course for me not to throw away a piece of paper that is printed only on one side.

In my memories of childhood, I often see myself with my mother. So I still vividly remember a winter evening, as I, the little girl, went through the snow holding my mother's hand. Her explanations at that time about the twinkling stars, when, in few words, she gave me an understanding of the vastness, the expanse and beauty of the firmament, left impressions in my child's heart, that I was able to understand only after many years. Today, I know that it was my mother's soul speaking to me at that time.

On this snowy, star-bright winter evening, as I stomped through the snow with my mother on the way home, she stood before the entrance to the house and turned her gaze up to the heavens, which was dotted all over with little, twinkling lights. I, the little girl, did the same.

She explained to the following effect: "The firmament," said mother, "is like a big tent that arches over us and is yet deep, wide and clear. Look up," she continued, "the stars are shining on us as if they want to greet us and tell us something."

I asked: "Is God above the stars?" And she answered: "They say that He lives above the stars. But I can't believe that, because in many situations, particularly during this time of war, I often feel that He is very near. But I'm sure about one thing, and I've experienced this myself in many imploring prayers to Him: He sees all of us – you and me. The stars are like eyes. They look at us and they shine especially clearly in the time before Christmas."

My question was: "Why especially before Christmas?"

Mother replied: "Perhaps through the big eyes of the stars God wants to say to us: Christ is born. Christ is resurrected. Pray to Christ – He helps. Perhaps through the rays of the stars, God wants to tell us: I Am the peace and you people should keep peace with one another."

Especially at Christmastime, we should think about the peace in the stable at Bethlehem.

There were often such and similar occurrences. Today I know that, without being aware of it, mother touched my soul. Even though the memory of such incidents paled at first, in my child's heart, in my soul, several fine strings had been touched and made to vibrate – we can call it sensitivity or religious sensation or experience.

Child, Say "Grüß Gott!"*

During my childhood, National Socialism ruled and encroached upon public life as well as the lives of individuals.

At that time in Germany, the "Heil Hitler" salute was in force. I can still well recall how my mother said to me again and again: "Say 'Grüß Gott' to our neighbors, to your teachers and to the priest."

I responded: "The teacher comes into the classroom and says 'Heil Hitler' and the city priest and the deacon also say 'Heil Hitler' and we children all have to rise, stand up straight and call 'Heil Hitler' and raise our hand in salute. How can I then say 'Grüß Gott'? I would get the yardstick rapped on my fingers."

Mother remained silent at this, but after a few days, she again instructed me: "Child, say 'Grüß Gott'!"

During my whole childhood, I saw soldiers in field gray and men in brown and black marching around. And during my whole childhood, I saw the priests in black robes and the teachers with the "Heil Hitler" salute, and my mother always said "Grüß Gott." She persevered with "Grüß Gott" and after the Hitler era continued to teach me "Grüß Gott" along with integrity and honesty. That's how it was and remained in our family.

* This is a standard greeting in Southern Germany that greets God in the other person.

Today as back then, the whole Hitler era was, and is, something suspect to me, belonging to a time in which I was still a child. My mother kept me away from this terrible ideology.

By the end of the war, the individual village, every woodlot and every hamlet in Germany was often defended. Also in the town where I lived, there were many antitank barriers. The result of this was that during combat actions, my parents' house, which father and mother had acquired through hard work, was partially destroyed. When father returned at the end of the war, he began to rebuild it. Everything was worked on and saved, until our house was rebuilt with persistent diligence.

In the time of transition from the end of the war to the beginning of a government life, a fairly long time went by with no school. This began again only after the greatest chaos was over. At that time, secondary schools existed only in the larger cities. During this time of extreme hardship, it was impossible for me to get there. Hardly any transportation possibilities existed. Trains and buses did have schedules, but they could rarely be kept, because tracks and streets had been bombed and repairs were being made everywhere, so that trains, in particular, were frequently late. Private vehicles were hardly available. Since attending a secondary school was out of the question, I entered occupational life after finishing elementary school.

Only rarely was there a firm that still functioned, because commercial activity was largely inoperative. Therefore, it was very lucky for a young person to get an apprenticeship in a firm after graduating. During this hard time after the war, my parents found an apprenticeship for me, so that I could begin training as an office clerk, which ended with the exam for being an assistant. With this, I had an occupation.

The war brought a currency reform with it. Money was scarce in all spheres of life. During this initial time of reconstruction, most apprentices were given their notice at the end of their apprenticeship. So after my exam for becoming an assistant, I lost my job. After several months, which I spent with my parents, I was able to start working as an office clerk in Munich.

Sense of Justice, Dynamism and Bubbling Vitality – the Expression of an Alert, Powerful Soul

When today, (1997) after nearly 23 years of the prophetic word, I look back at my childhood and adolescence, it is evident that even though I led a very normal life externally, already during childhood, there were, however, indications of a strong soul, whose strength radiated through its shell, the person, and was expressed in many ways.

I was very dynamic already as a child. Not that I was restless; I was constantly alert and ready to be put to use and do some constructive activity. There was a power in me, an energy that constantly pushed to be developed. I could never be placid and simply go with the situation. I could never turn a blind eye to what was uneven; I was never satisfied with what was incomplete, disharmonious or at a standstill, which could be developed and taken further, solved and beautified. I always had to face the situation, to make the best of the immediate circumstances.

Already early on, I demonstrated an exceeding awareness of justice. I denounced every injustice, whether in the family, at school or at work. Here, too, I did not want to be satisfied with what was uneven, imposed, and unequal. So I had a kind of nonconformist tendency, a rebellion against what was not right and just, and was ready and willing to work with all my strength for what I had recognized as right.

Viewed from today's perspective, I realize that my soul was striving for unfoldment and justice. The child put this urging of the soul into practice in dynamism, also in sports and every kind of activity. Already as a child I was physically very strong. I was the first to climb the cherry tree even though I was a girl. No tree was too high for me. No river was too deep or too wide to swim across. I undertook many bicycle excursions and was always one of the first in sports and games. So there was an unimaginable strength in me, which, unconsciously to me, trained my body. Thanks to the good relationship with my parents, thanks to the understanding and tolerance of both, and thanks to my mother's kindness and big-heartedness, this strength was never pressed into rigid forms and rules; the free way of thinking was not hindered; the free will remained unbroken. So I can say that I was a vitally alive child – and ultimately, this vitally alive child is still in me.

Today, I know that it was the strength of the soul, which expressed itself through the body and also trained the body for the prophetic office, because a person in service of God needs the appropriate physical constitution to be able to fulfill the manifold tasks from early till late.

So I was a quick child with a lot of temperament. I could laugh a lot, was very merry and already as a little girl, I always wanted children around me. However, I was reserved and shy among a lot of people. Often, I was not able to tell people something. Also later, the inhibition to communicate in a large group was for me a great hurdle, which had to be cleared to fulfill the office of prophetess and emissary of God.

In this, it becomes clear how widely spanned was the bow under which I had entered this life on Earth, how great the contrasts that came together in the human being Gabriele, with the soul dwelling in her.

But let us consider these facts in the light of God: He, the great Spirit, needed the strength, the dynamism as well as the reserve. Both were present in the genetic disposition and could later become channeled to prepare soul and person for the prophetic office.

For Church Christians, God Is Far Away.
"Sadly, God Cannot Hear Me …"

What was my attitude toward God during childhood and youth?

When I look back at that time, I realize that already then my soul resisted accepting the dogmas and rigid external forms of the church institution.

My parents were Catholic and, through my baptism as an infant, so was I. We knew no more about God than what dogma and rituals prescribed for us. We knew the Ten Commandments, but these were never brought home to us in such a way that we should apply them in daily life. During childhood, I went to church primarily at the hand of my mother. As a growing young person, I was advised, and often ordered, by my parents to attend mass.

When I recall my youth in pictures, I see myself as a Catholic sitting on the churchbench in rank and file with other young people to hear the sermon. The sermons offered me little, in many cases, nothing. My thoughts were elsewhere, or I fooled around with the young people who sat to the right and left of me, to pass the time.

When I bring to mind the thinking and feeling of the child Gabriele, as well as my prayers at that time, I realize with certainty that at the age of eight or nine, I had a very deep relationship with the eternal Father in heaven. I prayed to Him mornings and evenings. I tried to pray into the heavens above, where the eternal Father was supposed to be, who, according to the Catholic faith conveyed to me, writes into a big book everything the individual person does or does not accomplish, and, based on this, metes out love and mercy or His corresponding punishment to this person.

Often I thought in my prayers: Sadly, God cannot hear me; He is far above the clouds, far away from me and has so much to do.

Particularly during the transition period from childhood to adolescence, I felt the longing for God. During puberty, when a person forgoes his parent's guidance and wants to develop his own world of thought, which often contains many secrets, I pleaded to God for answers and help. As in the life of most young people, I, too, had situations in which I felt forsaken, in which I thought my parents did not understand me and I had to confide in someone who was more competent. I often expressed this concern in my prayers, and implored God for answers and help.

I would have liked to have received an answer to the many questions I brought to Him in prayer, but none reached me. We were taught not to hope for an answer from Him. Therefore, in my world of thought at that time, which was brought home to me in religion class, God was and remained far away, unreachable and unfathomable.

That frequently triggered great sadness in me. My prayers were about very personal things as well as difficulties, questions and problems of others, because during and after the war, anxiety and suffering were great, and there were many things I came into contact with.

Again and again, I asked the question about God, but my mother, my father and my grandmother could not answer these questions for me as comprehensively as I had expected. No one really knew where God is, what God is, how He is and if He exists at all. Since in religion class, these questions weren't also concretely answered, they remained open.

What was implanted in my child's heart, for example, through eternal damnation, broke out during my adolescence. This developed into an unimaginable fear of eternal damnation. The unforgivable that God is supposed to have imposed on me started to take root in me. What grew from this was a rejection of God, who supposedly would arbitrarily avenge Himself on me. Because no one could tell me who or what God is, because I hadn't learned to understand God, my Father, to the extent that I had brought out in my prayer concerns, I ultimately rejected God. Because of the doctrine of eternal damnation, I felt Him to be worse than all the vengeful and murderous people. You can move some people to change their behavior – but supposedly you cannot move God to rescind the eternal damnation that He speaks over you, not even when you feel remorse for your offence and no longer want to do it?

Another fear pervaded my youthful lack of understanding: After my death, my human person was supposed to rest in the grave as a moldy something or other, until the trumpets call me to resurrect in the flesh.

This is how the time went by from childhood to youth. I attended the worship services, but, as stated, mass offered me little. At about eighteen years of age, I essentially said the following to my mother: "I will no longer go to church. I can hardly relate to what is said and preached. I would rather go to the cemetery during this time to pray for the souls, just as we were taught, for the 'poor' souls."

My mother was raised in dogma and believed that one must go to mass at least once a week.

What most Catholics still believe today – that God is either in the church or in heaven – that was also my viewpoint back then. At eighteen, I did not yet know that each person himself is the temple of the Holy Spirit and that God can therefore be found in the innermost part of a person's soul. The nearness of God, the Spirit of the Eternal in soul and person, the divine love, which is closer to us than our arms and legs, was not taught to us.

In the end, many young people grow up as pagans or atheists, or they fall for idolatry, by worshiping human idols and following them. Even though the church institutions use the word "Jesus" or "Christ," I soon had to realize that they do indeed use the great name of redemption, but themselves do not practice what Jesus taught us and lived as an example. If we look deeper into the words "Christianity" or "being Christian," then we can deduce the following: Many call themselves Christian, whether, however, they are Christian, by following Jesus, the Christ, through the step-by-step fulfillment of His teachings, is anyone's guess.

First Years of Marriage and Relocation to Würzburg

During childhood and adolescence, my life was also like that of other young people. My nature was lively and vibrant; I didn't like sitting around doing nothing. There was a spirited adventurousness in me. I took every opportunity to bring something into movement here and there, to develop activities, including sports and such things. Now and then I read novels, but never scientific, religious or esoteric books.

Shortly before I started my job in Munich, I met my future husband, Rudolf. He was studying mechanical engineering and economics in Munich.

While I was working in Munich, we both had to economize. I still remember this time very well: For example, if we wanted to attend the theatre or a concert, we had to save up the money for it. That meant that we left out a meal now and then.

As a student, my future husband ate at the university dining hall. Sometimes he took me along, because there you could eat the cheapest. We always had to economize, in my parent's house as well as in my youth and in Munich. To be able to draw from material abundance is something I did not, and do not, know.

After we married in 1955, we found a small apartment in Munich. Because many houses had been bombed during the war, there was still a great lack of apartments. The currency reform had also taken place. A construction cost subsidy had to be paid for every apartment. For the small apartment of one and a half rooms, we had to come up with the then very high amount of three thousand DM. My husband was a refugee and had a claim to this amount. So we paid for the apartment, but did not have a single mark for ourselves, personally. For us, as a young married couple, this meant working together for our sustenance and for the rent. Thus, we gradually created the external conditions for a family.

From the beginning, our marriage was good; it was based on trust. We had many things in common and therefore did many things together. The annual vacation was also planned together and saved for. Like my childhood and youth, my life as a young woman proceeded like that of most other people.

Our daughter was born after about nine years. It was again a new step in our life together. I gave up my job. When our daughter was two or three years old, we rented a small, attractive townhouse in Munich, with a garden so that the child had freedom of movement. My husband and I were very economical, and thus we lived quite well. My husband rose steadily in his profession. As an industrial engineer, he had a good profession with upward mobility.

Very gradually, Germany emerged from the crisis of war and the post-war period. The shops filled with groceries, with clothing, furniture and much more. From the joy of leaving behind the years of privation, in many people – also in us – the desire grew more and more to have a vacation in neighboring countries and to be able to buy what had been impossible until then – or could be acquired only with considerable effort and austerity.

Things again moved slowly upward in all branches of industry. The automobile branch first produced small cars, then medium-sized cars and then larger ones. We also purchased a small car at first and then later a medium-sized one, to be more mobile and take trips. There were many opportunities to go on excursions around Munich. We frequently visited my parents. Distance meant nothing with the car. So a friendly relationship was formed through the visits and shared interests.

Having lived through the war and post-war years together, a warm, sisterly contact developed between my mother and me. We hardly kept any secrets from each other; we shared joy and suffering with one another, the sunny and less sunny days of life. A very friendly bond also developed between my mother and my husband.

In 1967 my husband's firm offered him a job in Würzburg. He was to take over a branch firm, develop and expand it.

This led to considerable disagreement between us, because my husband was immediately ready to accept the offer, while I did not want to leave Munich. I considered the city on the Main River to be a small town. Besides, we had rented the townhouse in Munich a relatively short time before, and we were also in the vicinity of my parents, whom, as I said, we visited very often. And so, I was opposed to Würzburg. With all the fibers of my being, I baulked against the move, as if sensing what I would be faced with there.

My husband, who was really looking forward to the new job, found an ally in my mother, who coaxed me to assent to this change of location, because it had professional advantages for my husband. She suggested that she visit us more often in Würzburg, or when we wanted to drive to Munich, to go via her town. Our daughter could then spend time there until we returned.

That was a powerful argument, because we had acquaintances and friends in Munich with whom we did many things.

My resistance diminished. My husband, Rudolf, coaxed me; my mother continued to influence me with practical arguments. We moved to Würzburg, unaware of what would come toward me.

2.
My Life in Würzburg Until the Breakthrough of the Inner Word

A New Rhythm of Life in the Quiet House in Würzburg

With the move to the city on the Main River, a new page was opened in the book of my life. Right from the beginning, the great all-wise Arbiter of all things and events steered a new course, as it were, toward a goal still unknown to me at that time.

The Gabriele of that time was still a human being like many others, but bit by bit changes occurred that set a new emphasis in my life.

At first, my husband was still working some days in Munich and therefore, I was often on my own back then. The human being Gabriele, whose inherent qualities were lively activity and dynamism, found the isolation from the pulsating city of Munich unfamiliar. Admittedly, there were house and garden to care for, but that still left quite a bit of leisure time. At first, I didn't know what to do with the hours of little to do. And the communication with my child did not offset the lively exchange with adult friends. I often felt lonely and initially suffered under this situation.

However, little by little I got used to the new rhythm of life in the home in Würzburg. I had lots of time and devoted myself extensively to our little daughter, who was exceedingly alert and enterprising, interested in everything and with a thousand questions.

Although during the initial time in Würzburg I was alone a lot with our daughter, I did not live in the tension and worry whether my partner – who travelled a lot – was faithful to me. I did not have this problem. I trusted him and felt linked with him, even when the one resided here and the other there.

Rudolf called me frequently, so that I shared in what preoccupied him; and I could telephone him at any time to report about me or our daughter and talk with him.

Thus far, my life ran its course harmoniously.

The Far-reaching Shock: The Surprising Death of My Mother. Does Life Go On?

Regular telephone calls with my parents, particularly with my mother, took place. I loved my mother, she was a great support to me in many situations. We always had lots to tell each other. For instance, we liked being creative in fashion, we took joy in furnishing the house and rooms, in taking walks through the woods and over the fields. We were interested in garden work, but also leisure hours and shopping expeditions in the city. Both of us loved autumn and winter, an introspective time.

My mother was likewise dynamic, strong and filled with zest for life. With her 62 years, she was interested in everything that was part of her sphere of life and sympathized with what moved her fellow people, joy and sorrow. People felt understood by her. She was not resigned, embittered and disappointed like many elderly people.

One day, after we had been living in Würzburg for about six years, a call from my hometown came from my brother who was fourteen years younger than me; he told me that my mother had a slight vein inflammation, but it was nothing serious.

We exchanged a few words, both assuming that this slight indisposition would quickly disappear. My mother also thought that she would feel well again in a few days, and so I saw no reason to visit her right away. Nothing indicated that she would leave this life so soon.

Today when I look back, I realize that this event had its harbingers. Weeks earlier, I had dreamed that my mother would die. I rejected this dream and thought no more of it. I did not want to preoccupy myself with death, because my nature was joy in life. My mother was mostly healthy, so I did not think of a demise.

However, it occurred in a different way and surprisingly. As death frequently enters many families without knocking, without asking whether it is alright with the person whom it calls – and with those it leaves behind – it also intervened in our family and fetched my mother overnight, as it were.

The occurrences around her demise take so much space in my descriptions because this event broke into my life like none other and induced me to think about life and death.

Now I experienced, lived through and suffered what countless unknowing people experience and suffer through with the death of a beloved person, who assume that this earthly existence is the life, the reality per se. Due to this ignorance, the death of a beloved person is an irretrievable loss. The Spirit, God, the life, often takes such events of shock, of a state of agitation, to make the person aware of the life beyond the threshold of death.

Severe illness and blows of fate are always indications, which, if the person recognizes them, can bring about a change in his life. That's how it happened with me. Only after years, did I recognize God's guidance in what back then seemed to be the greatest misfortune.

As an unknowing Catholic back then, I asked myself what meaning life is supposed to have! Where is God? Does God exist at all? Just like many people who stand at the deathbed of a beloved person and think about their ties and partings, so it was for me, too. The thoughts came again and again: This cannot be. A person cannot leave without saying goodbye. But death does not ask – it frequently comes for the person concerned without knocking.

The death of a beloved person always brings about inner movement and shock. The reaction that was triggered in me probably brought about a higher sensitivity, for I felt as if I heard an answer, which essentially said: "Child, I am not this shell. It is not the life." – At the same time, I thought I saw my mother standing in the room alive.

Another key experience could have let me realize at that time that life has no interruption. When the casket was being carried out of the house, I quietly murmured: "Oh, mother, you lived and worked in this house. You had to work a lot. How often was it all about pennies, our daily bread. Now, when things would have gone fairly well for you and father, you are being carried out of the house, in which you have worked and borne so much!"

Again I thought I heard the answer: "Only the shell, my child, not the life."

I didn't pay much attention to these incidents. They were overshadowed by my grief over her death. Today, I realize that these experiences were concessions from the divine kingdom. I was allowed to see my mother's soul, so that my soul could break open like nature in spring and soul and person could become more sensitive to the true life. Today, I know that this occurrence caused a real flood of questions to break open in me, the compulsion to get on the track of truth.

Questions After Questions About the Contextual Meaning of Life and About God

Never before had I been directly confronted with death. My turmoil caused me to look at my life and the life around me with new eyes.

During the subsequent five years, the following questions kept coming up in me again and again: Why do we actually live? Why the many blows of fate, the many situations in life? The one is rich, the other poor; the one comes into the world sick, for the other, things go well his whole life long; for still another, things go badly in this or other ways. What's that all about? Is that the life? What meaning do the contrasts, the ups and downs, have in our life? Does life consist of the pathways of our blows of fate, to which we are helplessly exposed? And what role does God play in this? Is human life a one-time life? What should a human life show me? Everyone has to die. Is everything over with death?

I also directed these and other questions to my acquaintances. I couldn't give myself an answer and my acquaintances couldn't either. On the contrary, they looked at me in amazement. Many a one shook his head and asked me: "What do you want with these questions? You live now. So, live! Why are you concerned about death? It will come sooner or later, anyway."

I was not satisfied with these answers. I continued to search. I had always been committed to unraveling the truth.

So now, too, I did not stop searching and asking, but I received no answer. Sometimes despondent, but often rebellious, helpless in my ignorance, I accused God and basically said to Him: "You, of whom many say that You are justice, truth, love, kindness and our Father, so if You exist: What kind of Father are You to bestow on us such a life? Nothing but work, economizing, worrying about our daily bread day after day! What about Your kindness and justice? A person slaves away year after year and when things begin to go better, he has to die – look at my mother. I find no trace of Your so-called mercy in this! Are You a God of love? Where should I seek you and how should I find You? How should I understand You? Where are You?"

Then again, I asked: Is there a God at all? Is there a life after this life? When is Judgment Day? How will we resurrect? Will we all live on the Earth again? Will we meet each other again? If yes: Will we recognize one another again? On Judgment Day, will so many people, as have existed during the entire history of humankind, find a place on our planet?

No one could give me a plausible answer. When I got answers, they didn't fit together.

All this triggered memories; pictures from childhood rose in my conscious mind. Again and again, I saw myself sitting in religion class hearing the priest teach us that all souls sleep until Judgment Day. While doing so, a thought formed in me again and again and ever more clearly: In nature there is no "end." In autumn, when the leaves fall, you can already see the new life; you already sense the new spring. During the passage of the seasons, what takes place is an emerging, a blossoming, maturing, bearing fruit, a withering of leaves and the start of new life.

What has roots, so I thought, doesn't die so quickly. Only when the roots are taken out of the ground, does the life wither and decay. Are dead people uprooted people, so to speak? Are they therefore buried until someday or other they again grow roots, to then resurrect?

Nature sleeps only briefly, for instance, in winter, and then it awakens again, mostly more lush and glorious than before. Nature has a life cycle, the coming and going – but soul and person are supposed to allegedly sleep endlessly, until the so-called call for resurrection comes?

My doubt in the theological-ecclesiastical doctrines could now no longer be pushed aside.

The Turn to the Spiritual.
An Inner Process of Realization

Many have experienced and continue to experience that once a person seriously and conscientiously begins to raise questions and to search for what is behind matter, and if he takes the Sermon on the Mount in hand now and then to read what Jesus taught us, then he can be seized by the Spirit of life, which – often by way of detours or seeming detours – guides him onto the path to the truth.

The soul dwelling in the person, which has awakened through the questions and search for the meaning of life, for what is behind the visible – because of a drastic event, often an illness, an accident or blow of fate – does not stop from pushing its person. In manifold ways, it urges him to question, to pray and to read the words of Jesus, so that the hard shell of the human ego becomes more permeable and the light is able to penetrate and brighten the soul as well as the person. The longing, the intuiting, the hope are forces that bring movement, so that God can guide His child.

The spiritual protector, whom we call guardian angel, which, as an invisible good friend, accompanies the person on his journey over the Earth, then becomes active via the conscience. Via the person's world of sensations and thoughts, it also tries to gently guide the person, so that he can recognize and take the next steps on his way to the true life. If the person's soul has awakened and if the person turns toward the true life, which is within, in all of us, then his spiritual protector can give answers to his questions. The person then receives tips, clarification and impulses regarding the truth in many ways, for instance, through seeming "coincidences," through situations or in conversations, through books and much more. According to the individual's state of consciousness and ability to comprehend, this occurs in an impersonal way, because the invisible, good friend is and works in the law of God; it always respects the person's free will.

So according to my soul's desire and mission, I was guided and led, at first indirectly with my questions, prayers and with my growing belief in God.
Insight added to insight. I simply accepted that we are children of God. Now I continued to deduce further: If we are children of an eternal Father, then we are from, and in, His eternal life. How can He, who is the eternal life, then again take the life from us over a shorter or longer period of time? He would never do that, because He would thus be taking a part of His own life and would be finite, because He would be a God of death in sections.
If my mother were alive, then I would see her again and meet her again. It suddenly seemed very logical: If she has eternal life, then I also have eternal life. Eternal life cannot be dead – life simply means life.

Again the picture of nature came to me. I realized with even more clarity: In reality, there is no standstill in nature; even though we say nature is sleeping, already in autumn life is forming itself into new and more luxurious abundance. It is in constant evolution. So, I thought, it must also be that way after the death of a person. Life continues in a step-by-step evolution.

In this way, the light of inner realization broke through more and more.

The questions about God, the life, preoccupied me ever more intensely and did not let go of me anymore, even when grief and anguish over the loss of a beloved person receded and the affirmation of life and activity again characterized my life. Through my questions about the meaning of life and my devotion to God, I received answers to many of my questions back then, but I did not know where the answers came from.

Inwardness Through Prayer. Nature, the Teacher

Nature became my teacher, because by way of parables, it showed me many interrelationships, which made our life on Earth more understandable to me. But I also discovered nature as a source of light and strength.

Without knowing what inwardness means, I was gradually led to a deep inner reflection of all things.

When I often stood at night before the house or on the balcony to look at the stars, again and again the intuition permeated me: God exists.

When I prayed the Lord's Prayer, I now spoke it more consciously. The words were no longer mere words. They now had a content; they were filled more and more with the sensation: God exists and so do all souls. However, I was not aware of where these insights and the firmness of knowledge came from: God exists.

One day spontaneous prayers bubbled out of me. I began to give thanks more than to make requests. From these prayers of thankfulness grew the certainty that God hears me, that He understands me, that He perhaps also embraces me and is my home.

Today I know that the bubbling prayers came from the depths of the awakened soul, which rejoiced that it was able to awaken its shell, the human being. These soul prayers made me free.

A new phase began in my life; I became calmer; the countless, erratic thoughts no longer ran through my conscious mind. The longing for diversion, the need for wordy exchanges in long conversations diminished.

Thus, stillness drew into me more and more. Again and again, I felt compelled to turn away from loud noises, to find my way into profound prayer, into a deep reflection of things. The picture of migrating birds flying to distant lands came to me. I, too, frequently felt the tug toward the stillness – into a land still foreign to me.

Even though I did not know what stillness means or what the inner life, the foreign land, would bring, I longed for it.

The Inner Experience: Life Continues after the Earthly Existence. There Is a God of Love

Indirectly, I frequently came into contact with my mother's demise, because every two or three weeks I visited my family, my father, who couldn't get over his wife's death. We took it on to comfort him, who seemed inconsolable and irreconcilable. From my father's point of view, my mother's demise was a tragedy into which he wanted to draw us children, my brother and me. Again and again, he blamed the doctor and was incapable of closing the void that had developed in his life through mother's death. He thought all people, including his daughter, were against him, because she did not respond to him as he would have wished. His complaints kept the wound fresh and he shut himself more and more into his dismal world of thoughts. At that time, he knew just as little about life after death as I did, because we had been brought up Catholic, that is, without the spiritual knowledge that could have been a help and support for us.

Father felt forsaken in his sorrow, the grief-stricken exclusiveness that none of us wanted to share. Appeals to reason, that life still went on and still held tasks and all kinds of nice things, did not reach him.

How many people react to the death of a beloved fellow person in such or similar ways! If they knew that with their sorrow, their pain, their entreaty of the deceased, whose soul they may possibly hinder from going forward – perhaps into more light-filled, beautiful worlds – then many would act differently. They would, perhaps after some farewell tears, let the beloved go on and leave it at that; by way of Christ, they would send him good wishes for his further path. Through this, they would also overcome the touches of pain and melancholy more easily and, apart from that, turn to the moments of their own life, which want to say many a thing to each one.

As it is the custom in Catholic areas, we drove to my hometown on the first anniversary of my mother's demise to visit her grave. Meanwhile, I had preoccupied myself with the many questions regarding life and death and, because of my reflections and insights about the cyclical course of life in nature, had come to the assumption that there is no interruption of life. For this reason, I had no real way of relating to my mother's grave. I went there more for my father's sake and because it was the custom.

When around noontime I was at my parents' house preparing for the walk to the cemetery, I had an experience that initially frightened me. I went through a small, bright room, looking through the window into the neighbor's garden, and my eyes and thoughts were again with nature. Suddenly I sensed that someone was in the room. I jerked around and clearly saw my mother standing there, smiling at me. It lasted only a moment, then the picture was gone.

I was briefly startled by this unexpected encounter. But then, I realized that for me this image was more real and said far more than all the reflection, questions and search for answers. It was immediately clear to me: That was her, my mother! And: She lives.

This firmly established in my consciousness the intuition and certainty about the continuation of life after death.

My many thoughts about life, which I had deduced from nature, were confirmed.

I knew that the inner perception of my mother was not a hallucination, for I no longer found myself in thoughts of mourning and heartache. I was active, full of eagerness concerning the questions about life. This experience in my parents' house brought me a solid answer to my many questions.

It was now clear to me that souls do not sleep until Judgment Day. There is a continual life; there is no interruption of our life.

For me, the following visit to the cemetery according to Catholic custom was not the visit to a dead person. Almost cheerful, I stood at the grave and felt happy with the experience that showed me the continuity of life. My father looked at me reproachfully, because he could not explain my behavior.

Much later, after the breakthrough of the prophetic word – more than four years after the death of my mother – I learned from the divine kingdom that this occurrence was another "concession" from the Spirit of God. These experiences served as a turning point in my life, to encourage the belief in God and the orientation to God.

Knowledge About the Meaning of Life on Earth. The Soul's Spiritual Potential Urges Toward the Light

All the answers to my questions about the meaning of life, all the inner pictures, insights and experiences brought about a rapid growth of my soul. It was the working of God, who thus drew me closer to Him. From the knowledge that there is no death, but continual life, merely in other aggregate states, I drew hope and the courage to believe in life after death and thus, in a God, who holds everyone and everything in His kind hands.

Once the to me important questions about God and the continuing life of the soul were answered, then at least a dozen more rose up in rapid succession. One of the most important was: What is the meaning of a material life? I pondered about this again and again, until several years after my mother's demise, a paperback book containing the screenplay "The Chips Are Down" by Jean Paul Sartre (Rowalt Publishing House) fell into my hands. I read it very quickly. Several statements about life after death and the return of the soul stayed with me and I suddenly knew that life in the beyond must run its course in a similar way as on this side of life.

This information animated not only my soul, but also me, the human being Gabriele. A certainty awakened in me – at that time I didn't know from where it came. It was clear to me: It must be similar and not otherwise: We are on Earth to discard our sins, to then return to God, who is the life, or to come back to the human existence.

Stimulated by the plot of the book, the certainty solidified in me: This God has created a gigantic universe; it must be an ingenious Spirit who knows each soul and each human being. Suddenly impression after impression opened up in me, pictures, contents of awareness, spiritual knowledge about vast cosmic correlations. To explain them here would by far exceed the scope of this book. Without having read or heard about spiritual correlations, without any information from outside – only from the impact of this paperback – I spontaneously knew that the soul continues to live in other worlds. In one moment I knew how it lives there, and that over and over again, the possibility of an incarnation is given.

This small paperback, which I had just skimmed through, made my soul vibrate, thus activating the truth in me. I could not, and cannot, prove the awakening of knowledge back then. But to me it was reality and later then became certainty.

Today, when I look back into that time, I can say that in the soul of a person lies the essence of the entire All, the truth. The awakened seeking soul receives the right impulse at the right time, so that the truth may break out in it, just as nature in spring.

Secretly, the preparation and ultimately, the spiritual schooling for the later prophetic office began.

With the germinating inner life, the doubt in God's existence and the accusations against Him melted away. Through the devotion to the All-Highest, I gradually found a hold in God.

During Prayer Meetings, More Impulses for My Inner Life. The Certainty: God Lives in Me! The Person Becomes Aware of the Soul's Knowledge

One day an acquaintance told me about a person through whom, as she said, the Spirit of Christ gave revelations during prayer meetings. The name "Christ" made me prick up my ears. I asked for the address. After several telephone conversations, during which I inquired if I could be present, this was granted to me. I went there and met about a dozen people who were praying. A woman spoke some things and it was said that it was Jesus. At first, it sounded to me like memorized words. I couldn't do much with it. Nevertheless,

I was drawn to these prayer meetings again and again at intervals of two to four weeks.

I listened attentively when I heard that the Spirit of Christ dwells in every person. Again I could affirm this – as if already eternally known to me – and felt very glad with the heavenly words. They fell into my soul like drops of water, of which my soul drank more than I, the human being, was able to understand.

The message penetrated my consciousness and I felt as though I had known it eternally: The Spirit of God dwells in each person, in all life forms of nature and in the four elements. Suddenly I become aware of the omnipresence of God. Now I had the evidence: I can find God and thus, Christ, in myself.

After I had overcome my initial skepticism, Christ's words effected many things in me, and it all began to stir in me. Everything was new for the human being, however, in the soul, the life broke open, as if a veil were suddenly taken away, and it entered my consciousness as a matter of course. One could say that all at once I was "in the know." It was a knowledge about the things of life, so clear, so concrete and certain, as though I had always known about it. I, the human being, of course, did not know it, and yet it was revived in me through the statement of the Spirit of Christ.

In other words: What high spiritual knowledge and spiritual strength lay in my soul remained unknown to my person as long as it stayed latent, that is, in abeyance. The words of Christ awakened this energy potential and it became active, rising from my soul into my conscious mind. There, it was now available to the person, who marveled at this, because in this life on Earth she had neither seen, heard nor learned anything like it. So, what was new for the person was for the alert soul clear eternity, truth from the stream of Being.

Today, after many years of the prophetic word, I clearly realize that God guided me to these devotional hours, so that I could attain the central knowledge that God dwells in me and that I am the temple of the Holy Spirit.

In this prayer group, I was called neither to the prophetic word nor to the inner word, nor instructed about anything else.

My spiritual growth took place "in the quiet chamber," that is, in the stillness, without the presence of other people. In the stillness, I was guided by the eternal light and prepared for the great work. In this way, I reached the inner being of my soul more and more, and the need for stillness, in which I felt close to God, continued to grow in me.

A Growing Nearness to God

In a relatively short period of time, my soul had developed much of its indwelling life, the spiritual potential of light. At first, my person could not keep up with this rapid development. I increasingly felt a discrepancy in my life and I longed to bridge it: On the one hand, was the knowledge about the pleasant things of life on Earth, and, on the other hand, a totally different kind of life opened up in my inner being, which I sensed was my true homeland.

With each foot I still stood in opposite camps, as it were, here within, there without. This caused tension and I longed to become one with myself. Ever more clearly I grasped that I could find myself only in me, myself.

Through inner tranquility, which developed ever more through a consistent alignment with the inner light, I increasingly gained inner strength. The gift to be able to see into many a situation and to clearly recognize what steps should be introduced to solve difficulties and problems gradually developed. I grasped situations, connections and causes in the blink of an eye.

When I now look back after many years, I can only give thanks, because all this and much more was a guidance that I merely sensed at that time. It happened to me and I did not know how.

Today I know that none of this happened by chance. I know how God's laws are effective in those people who devote themselves to the Eternal, but I also recognize which effects can develop from created causes.

During that time, the quiet time of preparation for the prophetic word of the Eternal, I frequently lay on the terrace during the summer months to enjoy the tranquility of nature. I watched the trees and became ever quieter. In this stillness, the relationship to the All-life grew ever deeper. This inner connection became more heartfelt, deeper and closer.

Despite this nearness to God, there were frequent fluctuations in my life. One time, I was pulled into my old habits, then again drawn more strongly toward the Spirit of the inner being.

Although my days were calm, at night in my dreams, I experienced that I was severely ill. In the morning, I could still remember the pain and fear, and how I struggled for health and much more. I took into my waking consciousness aspects of what had moved me in my dreams; so I had to deal with it and overcome it.

Despite these extremely opposite experiences during the day on the one hand, and during the night on the other, the desire remained to sit myself down to pray in the morning. I sensed that from the prayers grew more inner strength and a deeper love for the Infinite One.

At that time, I was not aware of it, but today I recognize that through the dreams and the inner struggles, through prayer and the struggle for stillness and peace, not only did my soul cast off more ballast, but my person also gradually refrained from what was unessential and all-too-human, in order to prepare myself to subsequently receive the inner light.

Harbingers of the Prophetic Word

Beginning with the demise of my mother, it took about five years before the prophetic word broke through. During these five years of inner awakening, I received spiritual gifts, insights into the divine life and, for my path, clear impulses regarding my world of feelings and thoughts.

While doing my housework, for instance, thoughts came regarding a small tree of life that had to become strong and therefore, had to be watered. However, I didn't attach any significance to these thoughts.

Later, when these impulses expanded more and more, when further teachings followed, I paused in my work and asked myself: Where do these clear thoughts come from, which are like words? Why am I preoccupying myself with a little tree of life? Such a picture has never before played a role in my imagination; I have never thought about a tree of life – what should this mean and where do these thoughts come from?

But again, daily life returned with joy and, again and again, with a fluctuating disposition. I didn't think any more about it.

Ultimately there were still more harbingers of the prophetic word, particularly during housework, when I was involved in activities that didn't need my full concentration. Once I was standing in the kitchen preparing a meal, when suddenly a short sentence entered my consciousness with penetrating intensity: *I Am the Lord, your God!*

This statement hit me unprepared. Had I produced this thought myself? In what connection? Well, it was familiar to me, because that's what the first commandment says, which I had learned in religion class. The words still reverberated in my consciousness, we could say that they resounded in me, as I went to the cellar to take the laundry out of the washing machine. And again came this sentence: *I Am the Lord, your God. You shall have no other gods before Me.*

Today I view this incident the following way: The Spirit of God was preparing His instrument. He plucked, so to speak, the strings of the harp that I should become, so that a small tone became audible now and then.

On a radiant summer morning in July 1974, my husband and I sat on the terrace flooded with sunlight having breakfast. We talked about my dreams, which deeply concerned me. Suddenly he seemed not to hear me. Unwaveringly, he looked past me; his awareness was elsewhere. I attentively watched his shining eyes. It seemed as if he was looking through me. Then he said: "I am a down-to-earth person and a clear thinker. I lead a firm; I have to specifically plan each day and make clear decisions, but what I just saw is beyond my comprehension."

And he said: "Behind you, I clearly and distinctly saw in the radiance of the sunlight a large, white figure with raised hands. To me it was and is Christ. What does this want to tell us?"

We looked at one another, reflective, moved, filled with questions. We could not explain this appearance. We sensed that we were under the care and guidance of the eternal Spirit. This was also substantiated by the words that had been given to me.

Everyday life returned and this occurrence was as if forgotten.

A week later, my husband and I were in the kitchen and I was again telling him about the dreams when he again saw the same image. Again, it was the light-filled figure that stood behind me. It could only be Christ, for the posture totally indicated Christ.

Disconcerted, we both remained silent for quite a while. I spoke reflectively, more to myself than to my husband: "What are we actually, as compared to the mighty universe? Nothing more than grains of sand."

Thereupon, words rose up in me, which were distinctly and clearly in my conscious mind and which I wrote down on a piece of paper. They were:

And this grain of sand, which you think you are, will, through My blessing, grow, flourish and bear exceedingly large and beautiful fruit, for the Lord is with you and will guide you into the land of love. Peace be with all of you. Amen.

These sentences were the first harbingers of the prophetic word, which almost a year later fully broke through.

A little later, in August 1974, I heard the following:

I Am the truth and the life. I will help and support the one who believes in Me and asks Me, also during the hardest times, which will break in over humankind. I hold My hands over My children in blessing.

Again, I wrote these words down, read them frequently and let them fall deep within me. My person trembled and could not comprehend it.

Everyday life blurred the impressions. God's words took a back seat. However, what I never neglected to do was to go into contemplation and prayer.

On Christmas Day 1974, a pronounced event took place again, which likewise indicated what was to come.

The holidays were harmonious; calm and relaxed, I sat looking at a wooden sculpture. Suddenly thoughts rose up in me, which were again like words: *I am your spiritual teacher, Brother Emanuel.*

Then it was quiet again.

When I told my husband this, we both shrugged our shoulders and left it at that.

Today, after many years, it is a certainty that all this and much more was the preparation for the great event, which later took place, the prophetic word, the word of God.

3.
My Path as the Teaching Prophetess and Emissary of God Until the Year 1997

*Breakthrough of the Prophetic Word.
First Lessons From Christ and From the
Divine-Spiritual Teacher Brother Emanuel*

On January 6, 1975, at about six o'clock in the evening, the inner door opened a crack to the spiritual reality, to the inner life. The inner light of revelation broke through and very quickly became a great stream.

From the sunroom of our house, I looked quietly into the garden. Suddenly an infinite stillness surrounded me. My thoughts were with my father in my parents' house and with the many situations during the past five years since my mother's death.

I started to pray and above all, to give thanks, also for the many events in which we were protected by an invisible hand, because my family and I often travelled by car, also to visit my father.

At the same time, I thought about sleeping nature, in which new life could already be seen. Suddenly to my left, I saw a beautiful figure, a being in a radiant white garment. My first thought was: That is my guardian angel.

As I thanked him, the following words fell into my inner being: *Peace and love are with all of you, the blessing of the Father and of the Son. God leads you on your pathways; God is your refuge and shield. The great One, the only One: Him we want to serve; Him we want to praise, and to Him are due all thanks, for He is the Father and we are all His children. Amen.*

The image of the being faded, but the words stayed clearly in my consciousness. I wrote these sentences down on a notepad that was on the table next to me. The words were powerful and loving; they conveyed hope to me.

From this, I gathered the courage to ask: Why am I so plagued in my dreams?

The answer in me was: *Everything that is in the soul turns to without. When the soul is cleansed, the divine irradiation can begin. Fear not! Confront these dreams with God's strength and love – and you will be the victor. We are placed at your side to protect you, and if you do everything in love, you will suffer no harm on body and soul.*

The Lord is with you – and His Spirit goes with you on all your paths. Do everything with the words: Jesus Christ is with us.

I also wrote down these words.

With this clear input of a coherent text from the divine world, the prophetic word had broken through.

Since that time, I receive the gift of divine revelation daily. For me, this great, mighty gift of grace came surprisingly, for I had never been concerned, that is, I had never deliberately tried, to hear something. I was happy in prayer, in the stillness and in meditative contemplation. From this, grew the strength that gave me hope and confidence as well as understanding and love for my fellow human beings.

God now spoke directly through the largely purified soul into the person – a process that I was now privileged to experience, the course of which, however, first had to be made clear to me by the divine realm. Through constant devotion and the fulfillment of the laws of God, I heard His holy word ever more clearly and deeply in me. Right after the breakthrough of the divine word came the first instructions from the Spirit of God, first from Brother Emanuel, who had introduced himself as my spiritual teacher, and then from Christ, the Spirit of God that revealed itself.

Thus, Brother Emanuel is my spiritual teacher and, at the same time, my guardian being. Bit by bit, I received from the eternal Being the explanation that Brother Emanuel had accompanied me from childhood on and also during several previous lives, to prepare me for the prophetic word and the divine teachings.

At first it was mere drops of divine impulses; soon after, however, a mighty stream of life flowed through my soul, which then formed itself into the divine word in me. My spiritual teacher spoke to me daily. I was totally free to receive him or not. He always said:

If it is your will, if you want to, then I would like to talk with you.

When Brother Emanuel spoke, there were always instructions, which at first lasted ten minutes, then a quarter of an hour; later it became half an hour and after that even longer.

These inner lessons from the Spirit of God at first mainly brought home to me the necessary basic spiritual knowledge. There were instructions concerning my personal life situation, externally and internally; there were answers to questions that were in me or that I directed to my spiritual teacher in my inner being; I received impulses, small exercises and tasks. More was built on the insights, the experiences I made, that is, the steps that I had taken. In the school of the Spirit of God, I learned to align myself with the divine prophetic stream and to practice concentrating on it.

Soon after the breakthrough of the holy word, a mighty voice of light rose in me, the words of which I wrote down. They were:

I Am Jesus Christ, the Redeemer of all souls.

I became frightened and wanted to stop the inner stream through a lack of concentration. Thereafter, came the loving divine rays of impulses in the words:

Do not fear! You are under My care, for you went forth from the kingdom of light to take in My word and to pass it on to the world.

Then the great warm light continued speaking:

O child of eternal love, I want to guide you to the great spiritual goal. Why do you hesitate? Write down the words of life that I bring to you daily anew, for you shall be active for Me. This is how it shall be, now and evermore. Believe in the voice of your heart and you will learn what I wish from you. Do you want to be the doer or the hearer of My word? The blessing is with you at all times. Amen.

Right after that came additional and mighty, enveloping impulses of light, which warmed me throughout and set me aglow.

So it said:

O children of the Earth, what you need is the sun, the light: The light of My spiritual sun, which envelops all life, which gives strength and peace. O take it in, this light, and pass it on to the many who long for this light.

The Voice of God Through the Prophet

The voice of God was and is unmistakable. It is strong in me and sublime above all else. This voice knows no ifs and buts. It is clear and expressive.

When I talk about the voice of God, then the word of Christ is also meant, for the Spirit of the Father and of the Son is the omnipresent stream, the word.

To be able to purely receive the voice of God, the soul of the person has to manifest a certain degree of purity. Thus, the love for God has to prove itself in the deed. "Deed" means to discard what the day shows the person in the way of sinfulness and to fulfill His commandments step by step.

The voice of God is light, the voice of the heart, which flows through God's instrument and is revealed in the prophet's native language.

The prophet is an interpreter of the holy light, of the holy voice, since God does not have the language of human beings. This is why a long preparation is necessary until a prophet of God can be effective. I was prepared for the prophetic office over several incarnations and at the same time, for the spiritual teaching office.

The Almighty revealed to me that this preparation took place over incarnations. As a human being, I have no memory of this. The Eternal spoke: *You can see from this, that in this life on Earth, a longer time of preparation for the breakthrough of My word was not required.*

Everything was prepared for this in the soul. What applied to me also applies to all prophets: A prophet's soul must be pure to a great extent. God's instrument has to have largely opened his spiritual consciousness through the insight and fulfillment of the divine laws, through a life of selfless love.

In this incarnation, it only took the impulse from without and the question to within – is there a God of love? – and then the time of preparation of stillness and prayer. Over the course of the years, the word became a mighty wellspring, a great stream that pours itself into all spheres of life. No sphere is excluded from this. The mighty Spirit of the Christ of God sets His impulses everywhere.

When a soul becomes pure, then it is linked more and more with the Absolute Law, God. When the soul immerses into the stream of the eternal law, into the Absolute, then it is permeated by the Absolute Law and has again become absolute, the eternal law, God. It is then divine.

People tied to mainstream churches do not understand terms like "selfless" and "absolute." They know and speak only the ecclesiastical language of the theologians, which does not go beyond the limits of their concept of God and church doctrine. In contrast, the language of the mystic, the language of a person who is turned within, which concerns the innermost being, is unknown to them, because the spheres of inner life are foreign to them. The church functionaries have in their vocabulary – and in what they comprehend and pass on – only the myth about Christ, but not the inner, the omnipresent, Christ of God, the Resurrected One, the power and the redemption, the light that dwells in all souls and human beings. They talk about the Creator and do not know about the Creator-Spirit, which is present in all things. They create for themselves a picture of Christ, of God, and convey this – and do not know the reality of the Christ of God, of the Living One, who dwells in each one of us; nor do they know the reality, God, who is the life.

My life became, and still is today, actualized prayer. At the beginning of the prophetic word, my spiritual teacher, Brother Emanuel, gave me some advice, which I heard many a time during the following months and years:
Align solely with the power of God! Pray so that your soul become stronger, so that it can perceive the holy light, the language of light, ever more deeply and comprehensively.

The path to the light, to the heart of God, is the Inner Path, which the Spirit of God teaches again today.
In this life, I did not walk the Inner Path as the pupils of the Inner Path walk it today. It was revealed to me that I had already walked this path in previous existences. I felt that my soul immediately grasped it, because right at the begin-

ning of the divine word the highest wisdoms were reflected to me, which I understood at once.

There is a divine mission behind every prophet. The prophet is prepared – by God and by a spirit being assigned to him by God – to receive and pass on the prophetic word.

A prophet is trained to be able to clearly and distinctly pass on the impulses of light. God's word simply flows through the prophet. He hears God's word without straining to hear. We human beings are responsible for each word that we speak, and so is the prophet, as well.

My Spiritual Teacher: Brother Emanuel, the Cherub of Divine Wisdom

A spirit being is placed at the side of the prophet-to-be as spiritual teacher. On the one hand, so that he will continue training until his soul and the individual aspects of his person are largely in accordance with the divine, so that they can receive the direct light, that is, until soul and person are attuned to the mighty All-Sender, God. On the other hand, the being that protects and teaches gives to the prophet-to-be impulses on how he should align himself and live, in order to become one with the inner light, so that he can receive the first impulses of light.

In my case, Brother Emanuel stayed at my side and is still there today, because he not only prepared me for the prophetic office, but is likewise responsible for the spiritual teachings.

In this respect, still today, he gives me protection and help, for the questions posed by my fellow people are not always clear. He taught me to recognize the ambiguity of the statements and to teach in an unequivocal way. Moreover, Brother Emanuel also provides for me with those tasks that behoove a guardian spirit, a guardian angel.

During the first months at the start of the training for the prophetic work, Brother Emanuel was simply my spiritual teacher and good friend, whom I quickly took to heart. I went to him not only when I had questions concerning my spiritual unfoldment, but also when worldly questions and difficulties came up. He always stood by me in word and deed, according to the laws of life.

Later I learned that the name "Brother Emanuel" is merely a name – a pseudonym, as it were – for us human beings, because the divine name of a pure being cannot be passed on with our words. I learned that Brother Emanuel, my spiritual teacher, is also the responsible servant of the Lord in His divine work. He is the Cherub of divine Wisdom, one of the seven law angels before the throne of God.

When I heard this, I was terrified. I was scared. Because I had not known of the greatness and might of this spirit being, I spoke with him in a very familiar way. It was all too exalted for me, the plain and simple person who wanted nothing more than to be God's eternal child. Following this, there was a brief interruption in the communication with Brother Emanuel.

In this situation, I turned to the Father-heart as a child, since the word "Father" meant to me protection, help, my homeland, a place of refuge, where I was secure, and still am to this day.

The divine kingdom showed understanding for my momentary reticence. During the following time, the Spirit of the Christ of God explained to me the connections between God-Father and Him, Christ, the first-beheld and first-born Son of the heavenly Father. Christ also explained to me His workings as Jesus of Nazareth and what significance His life on Earth had, and has, for the present and coming time. Christ instructed me in the spiritual laws and helped me to keep them.

After some time, Brother Emanuel approached me from within just as friendly and kindly as before and again took over the teaching function.
Thus, I was again informed about the spiritual laws that are behind the circumstances and processes in matter, about the pure heavens, about the Fall of the once pure spirit be-

ings and about the Fall-worlds, which became spheres of purification through the Redeemer-power of the Lord, and much more.

After being taught for some time, I, the human being, received another shock. Cautiously and gently, Brother Emanuel helped me to understand that – as I already mentioned – my incarnated spirit body comes from the region of light of the Cherub of Wisdom, and he explained the following spiritual principle to me:

Once the soul on the path to the divinity has reached a high degree of purity, then a spirit being from the divine home region assumes the protection for this soul and this person.
Thus, I learned that Brother Emanuel is not only my spiritual teacher and my guardian being, but is also the positive principle, the dual-principle, of my incarnated spiritual being. When I grasped these connections, it came as a shock which I had to come to terms with.

Very gradually, I learned from Brother Emanuel that during the history of humankind, spirit beings from the heavenly Being frequently incarnated.

After many years of the prophetic word and countless divine revelations, in which the Almighty gave His highest teachings through me, His instrument, I can say that this announcement was too much for me at that time. The soul had understood it, but the human being could not comprehend, because I felt, and feel, myself to be a plain and modest person, who strives for only one thing: to convey the justice of God and the truth of the Being to people just as it is the will of God. I was, and am today, nothing but His instrument, His handmaid, His maidservant. His will takes place in me and through me.

Today I know that what occurred over the course of many years was good and useful for my soul, because the soul and person grew more and more into the will of God. According to the degree of maturity, the Spirit of God and Brother Emanuel could reveal to me the inherent laws of life and their correlations. The entire preparation from the Spirit of God, the spiritual ethics, the development of higher and high moral values and above all, the suffering that I bore, because I, the human being, did not want to accept many a thing – all this, particularly the suffering and then again the glorious revelations, led me into even greater humility and the renunciation of all human sinfulness.

In connection with the terms "human" and "sinful," I want to explain the following: In the mystical language, the "human" is the sinful. The "human being" is the body; it is the expression of the soul, that is, the shell that surrounds the spiritual substance. When the human being sins, he often turns away from ethics and morals – he becomes unprincipled. In the mystical language, this means that he sins. That is "human."

During the training instructions, Brother Emanuel again and again attentively gave me advice to the following effect:
Align solely with the divine stream and with me, your teacher, who lives in the divine power and is assigned by the Spirit of God to directly attune you to this holy stream, so that you are able to receive ever deeper wisdoms from the one inner source.

Later, the Cherub of divine Wisdom conveyed to me that he lifted, and lifts, the truth of life from the soul's core of being, to then put it into our three-dimensional words, that is, into the prophetic word.

Again and again, it was said:
Pray, and be aware that the human being of itself is not capable of fulfilling God's works. You shall serve your Lord and master solely as a vessel. The more you, the human being, submit and give the divine life the possibility to align you with the inner wellspring, you will find inner peace, joy and harmony.

And so, I grew toward being God's instrument. He, the great Spirit, instructed me to bring His holy word of light to

His human children. After all the many years of prophetic activity and all-encompassing service, I humbly and thankfully profess: I know that I, solely the human being, know nothing unless the love and wisdom of God speak through me.

The Great Task: a Worldwide Work. Notification of Attacks, Defamations and Persecution of Christians

Ever more details about the spiritual life and about the great worldwide work, which was being prepared and is now worldwide, were revealed to me by Christ, the Redeemer and Savior of all souls and fulfilled human beings and by Brother Emanuel, my spiritual teacher. The eternal Spirit, God, revealed to me everything that I needed to know for the future of the divine work.

Among other things, it was revealed that the church leaders do not lead people to God in the innermost being of the person, but to external forms, to cult acts, to rites and ceremonies and thus, to external temples. It was explained to me in detail that all this is not necessary, because the fulfilled person, himself, is the temple of the Holy Spirit.

The light spoke:

The human being does not need the external cathedrals and palaces of the churches; he does not need an external Holy of Holies – in himself, he has the light and thus, the Holy of Holies.

Christ and Brother Emanuel made me aware again and again:

You are the temple of the light. Awaken the light in you more and more, so that the voice of the Eternal can comprehensively speak through you and so that His Spirit can comprehensively work through you.

The light, which is the word, explained further:

Because many souls in the astral worlds, that is, in the purification planes, are unknowing and still feel bound to external forms, they only rarely accept the teachings of God's messengers. Many do not listen to the truth; they continue to seek God in the external world.

Christ, the inner light, explained to me:

I love all human souls – and go especially after the lost sheep, which, among other places, can also be found in the denominations. Above all, they are those who aggrandize themselves in My name, who bind My sheep, their believers, to their narrow doctrines and ideas, thus keeping themselves, too, in seclusion from the eternal light for an endlessly long time.

The eternal light in me continued to speak:

I also want to turn against the Satan of the senses, who has made himself at home particularly in the denominations. I want to clarify and be effective, so that the souls in the purification planes, too, come to their senses and let go of their inclination toward the Earth, because on the Earth many people are bound to external forms through the irradiation of souls that believe in the church.

After several months of the divine word, the Spirit of the Eternal spoke about the worldwide work in more detail. The Eternal said:

I want to give to the nations of the Earth all the wisdom, the whole truth of infinity, to the extent that it can be expressed with human words, so that the many seeking people receive many seeds from the eternal wellspring and water them with their faith, so that they open and sprout in the heart, and soul and person find their way to the light, to the truth, and through this, can grasp still far greater truths.

When I think back on my youth, I have to say about myself that I became shy when I had to speak to a lot of people. Before the prophetic word it would have been absurd for me to even think of speaking before thousands. Back then, I would have said: I cannot do that because I'm not trained for it. However, when the holy voice set me aglow, all these arguments became futile, for the eternally loving Spirit gently guided me, step by step, into the divine prophetic mission. He did not ask too much of me, but carried His plan through – in the rhythm that is foreseen. In this plan, in this work, which can be compared to an enormous clockwork, in which many wheels intermesh, I was and am one wheel. However, if this wheel did not want to operate in the rhythm of the eternal plan, that is, if the human being rebelled, then the wheel was stymied, because the clockwork continued to run as foreseen by the great cosmic master. What was left for the little wheel to do other than to come to its senses?

The Eternal explained to me – insofar as I could absorb it back then – everything that would take place during the following years. He said that many people who recognize the truth would come to me. But that many people will also come into His work, who merely give the impression of being there for Christ, but then leave when they cannot push through their material goals. Besides that, the great Spirit spoke of the attacks by the institutional churches. He said that I would be disparaged and slandered, that many church leaders, who do not live the words in their Bibles, would persecute with character assassination those who stand by the Christ of God, the life.

When I heard all this, I became anxious. But the light in me was stronger. The loving power that enveloped me, that protected and carried me, conveyed security to me, so that I also accepted these announcements.

The Eternal's voice also revealed that these violators of God's law would expose themselves through their defamations, mockeries and malicious slander. He spoke of a modern persecution of Christians, during which swords and lances would no longer be drawn to slaughter those of other faiths, but would be carried out with the pen and paper of journalists. God also spoke of the press, radio and television, which in many cases are servile to the leaders of the churches and therefore spread unverified untruths that are disseminated by church leaders. So even today His words still apply: *If they have persecuted Me, they will also persecute you.*

I indeed heard all this; the Eternal kept nothing from me. Nor did He keep from me that all this would be suffering, grief, worry and bitterness for me.

So I was aware of what would come toward me, because it was told to me clearly and distinctly. But my person ultimately grasped what it specifically meant only when it could be felt firsthand, as it were, on my own body. Then my soul's fight against the reluctant human being again began – the yes to God had to be achieved by the human being again and again.

One time given, it cannot be taken back again; it becomes the law for the person. The yes has a great effect again and again; it has to be fulfilled at some point. To give the yes was relatively easy. But great tests were yet to come to me.

The Rapid Growth of the Divine Work. Steadfastness and Strength for the Life and Work in the Spirit of God

Even when the soul has been intensely prepared during several incarnations for its future task, the path to the prophetic office is the hardest work, as it were. Everything that is turned without – the old habits, the all-too-human aspects, which permeate the whole person and shape the consciousness of every cell of the body – has to transform, so the inner being, the strengthened soul's potential of light and power can radiate to without, that is, can illuminate and flow through the person, so that the human being gradually corresponds to the vibrations of the soul.

In addition to the struggle to be free of my own familiar human aspects, the struggle came increasingly with adversities that, from without, afflicted the work of the Eternal and me, as well. Thus, only bit by bit did I become aware of the dimensions of what I had said yes to and at the same time, had assumed the responsibility before God. I learned all that was in store for me.

There were more and more divine revelations to be given before people. At first it was a small circle of friends, then the Spirit of God led more brothers and sisters to us, who recognized the Eternal in His word and were willing to support His work, which at the beginning He called "The Homebringing Mission of Jesus Christ."

The first brochures appeared in the simplest form; individual divine revelations were typed up and copied, distributed, as well as flyers, for instance: "Christ Speaks Again."

At the request of the Spirit of God, we rented medium-sized public rooms and placed advertisements in the newspaper. The Eternal gave revelations – at first, before many empty chairs and only a few people – in moving words about the heavenly homeland, about our eternal Father, about the beings of light and about the great cosmic correlations. He likewise brought home to us the basics of the divine inherent laws and above all, the fundamental details of the law of cause and effect. Again and again, Christ spoke of a great, worldwide work – but patience, many prayers and many a selfless effort were still needed for a long time, before the rows of chairs in the halls began to fill after many months.

The work grew rapidly. Christ-cells, the predecessors of the Inner Spirit=Christ Churches, developed in Germany and abroad. Soon large events with great revelations of God took place in many cities in German-speaking countries and in the course of great journeys to give revelations in the rest of Europe and overseas. Books with divine revelations were extensively published; further books by Christ-friends were added to this.

Further and Deeper Training by My Spiritual Teacher, Brother Emanuel. The Step-by-Step Guidance Toward the Absolute Consciousness

The eternal Spirit successively guided me ever deeper into the way of thinking of my fellowman. In this way, I very gradually came to understand how other people feel, sense, think, how they talk and act, and recognized what was behind their feeling, sensing, thinking, talking and acting. This perspective made me strong for living and working in the Spirit of God.

Since the beginning of the prophetic word, I feel the presence of the divine kingdom. It is the communication, as it were, between the primordial essence of being, the incorruptible Spirit, the largely purified soul and the human being aligned with God.

Through this communication, which is a subtle sense of the presence of the Being, and feeling into people, into the words and behavior patterns of my fellow people, I have become very sensitive to my surroundings. The divine consciousness in me, which radiates through the person, can be compared to a huge radar screen that takes in the various kinds of vibration of my surroundings, which I can then also interpret.

Through this sensitivity, I have also gained self-control over my behavior. It is the fine senses that are aligned with the divine that help to form the so-called radar screen. If I digress from the divine communication and go into thinking patterns that are not desired by God, then I immediately feel the intensified radiation of the divine kingdom. At the same time, I have pangs of conscience. Brother Emanuel, my spiritual teacher, who respects the free will to a free decision, then gave, and gives, me impulses, so that I check my behavior, to then promptly rectify what does not correspond to the will of God, which is also the will of my soul. The love for the eternal Father gives me the strength to clear up the wrongdoings that arise and to devote myself to the One whom I faithfully serve.

A part of the inner perception of divine reality is also the fine sensory perception, which can also be called clairsentience. For instance, I feel the dullness of people in a room who talk a lot and think even more. However, when I perceive the divine in me, then it is like a heavenly fluidum, or aura, which stimulates the soul and the heart, which conveys to the soul, but also to the person, a feeling of lightness, joy and closeness, which cannot be described in words.

The divine training through Brother Emanuel, the Cherub of divine Wisdom, continued.

He taught me that God speaks out of countless mouths – out of all the components of nature, from each atom, from each animal, from the elements and the heavenly bodies, from every cell of the body and from every particle of the soul – because God, the eternal Spirit, is present, eternally revealing Being. I learned that the powers of creation in nature are the energies of evolution that lead all the forms of the nature kingdoms to further development. He taught me to perceive the life of creation deep in my soul.

Just as I hear the prophetic word, I experience that all of nature, the whole Earth, yes, all of infinity is the mighty garden of God, which is constantly revealing itself. Thus, I learned that the life of evolution flows out of the great Creator-source, and that in the eternal Being, in the four regions of evolution of eternity, in the natures of God – Order, Will, Wisdom and Earnestness – the spiritual body of every spirit being is built up.

The spiritual development takes its course via the heavenly mineral, plant and animal kingdoms up to the matured nature being, which is raised to filiation by the Father-Mother-God through the three filiation attributes of Kindness, Love and Gentleness, thus becoming the child of God, the pure being, the microcosm in the macrocosm, the All-Being.

These teachings were the beginning of a new, even deeper training. The divine lessons, which I received via the prophetic word, among other things, concerned the four spiritual elements, the make-up of the five kinds of spiritual atoms as well as the structure and quality of the spirit body of the pure beings and of the soul. At that time, I, the human being, had no idea of all these glorious interrelationships in the eternal Being, but, with dedication and forbearance, my teacher understood how to again open up for me the knowledge about these all-encompassing inherent laws of the inner life, the evolutionary steps in the Being and the make-up of the eternally divine structures.

To convey all these details of the eternal laws, Brother Emanuel had to use elements from my vocabulary, which he struck, as it were, like a pianist would strike the keys of his instrument, because the divine kingdom does not have the language of human beings.

When I look back at the beginning of the prophetic word, I am frequently touched in my heart by the devotion, love, kindness and patience with which the great Spirit of life gave me an understanding of the smallest divine spiritual principles, which, at the same moment, I became aware of in pictures.

The unknowing person that I was back then had no idea, for instance, about the All-streaming of the eternal Spirit, God.

If he wants to grow closer to God, every person – no matter what he calls himself – has to put God above all else. Nothing may be more important to him than to fulfill God's will.

Anyone who does not heed the first commandment – *Love God, your Father, with all your heart, with the depths of your soul, with all your senses, with all your strength and your neighbor as yourself* – cannot receive God's word. I had to learn that. However, that is not to my credit. This is due to the divine kingdom that constantly taught and instructed the willing human child.

Honor, praise, glory and thanks are due solely to the One, who is the love Himself: God, our eternal Father in Christ, our Redeemer.

To Be a Prophet
Is the Call and the Calling by God.
Soul and Person –
A Prisoner in Service of God

It took several years of struggle, until the harp was attuned to God and could, and can, be used by Him totally according to His will.

So, as I gained victory over myself with the help of the Spirit of Christ, the channel of revelation widened, so that by way of the harp of the opened spiritual consciousness, God was able to reveal the symphonies of the seven basic powers, the primordial powers.

This is the all-encompassing revelation of the eternal Being, as far as the truth can be passed on with human words.

At the divine calling, the Eternal spoke to me according to the following:

Out of love for Me, God, the Eternal, you have freely assumed this difficult office and freely went into the depths of the Fall-realms, to become a human being and fulfill this mission.

You freely went into density, into limitation, into lack of freedom and peace – into the realm of shadows, where you come into contact with all the shortcomings of the human ego.

Besides that, it was explained to me that the mission, to serve the Eternal on Earth and the people as a prophet of God, is in abeyance in the soul until God calls the prophet. And so, God determines the point in time in a life on Earth at which He leads the human being away from the worldly tasks, and places him in His calling. With the breakthrough of the prophetic word, this was revealed to me and the question was directed to me, the human being, whether I would now accept the mission of the soul.

Until the divine mission has been fulfilled, the person, whose soul bears the prophetic office, has only a certain potential of free will. His yes, given to the Eternal, has to be honored, that is, fulfilled.

It is true that initially I could have said no. But even when the human being does not say yes right away, then certainly in later times, because the yes in the eternal Being is binding. The mission engraved in the soul compels, as it were, the person to do what the task entails.

When I look into the time of the calling, then I realize that I did say yes, however, it was not the person who gave this yes, but the soul, which overpowered the person. Today I can say that when the time is ripe and the yes to God has matured, soul and person can do nothing but say yes, because, if the yes has to be fulfilled at this time, both are prisoners, as it were, in service of God.

Several times I wanted to withdraw from the mighty mission, which from the first hour of the prophetic word came at me massively and often seemed to overwhelm me – but not from the yes that the child gave to the Father of love, to fulfill His law, the holy light, in order to be totally in His holy nearness.

The yes of the child of God to the Father did and does endure. The yes to the mighty mission, that the human being became aware of again and again, often fluctuated between yes and no, and yet the yes was an integral part of this mighty mission.

There were times when I, the human being, thought I could not measure up to the great event, which the Spirit of the Eternal had announced through me and which was taking shape more and more. However the inner light did not accept these arguments and ideas.

The unending love of a spirit being for God, its eternal Father, cannot be grasped by the human being. The person himself would not accept such a complex and serious mission.

The human being Gabriele speaks: "My whole life changed. It became a life of privation, of suffering, a life in which I was scorned, reviled and mocked, the life of a woman over whom all kinds of abuse were poured, above all, by the so-called Christian churches. In order to do justice to God's mission, I had to give up everything that was near and dear to me as a human being, in order to be totally there for the Eternal and for my fellow human beings. The only beauty that remained is the deep connection between the eternal Father and me, His child, and the selfless serving, the drawing from the eternal wellspring for my neighbor."

To Live in the World, But Not With the World. The Teaching Prophetess and Emissary of God

After several years of prophetic activity, I sensed how my soul very gradually immersed in the eternal stream and became one with the Eternal through the daily actualization and fulfillment of the eternal laws.

The unification of the soul with the eternal stream, God, is the highest feeling of happiness. This becoming one of the soul with the Eternal can hardly be described in words. In the human being, it is a constant flowing and streaming, the nearness to God, which brings about an indescribable sense of secureness, of safety and a feeling of being alive that cannot be described with human feelings. It is an inner process, a feeling of being carried and the awareness of being at home in the All. Time and space disappear.

The human being, who is the shell of the soul, can experience only in fragments what this means for the soul, to have returned home to the cosmic Being.

Once the person's soul has immersed in the eternal stream, in the eternal wellspring, then it is largely pure and is in constant communication with God. The person's brain cells that are oriented toward God are like a ladle, with which the person can tirelessly draw from the stream of the Being.

Of course, the human being himself, whose soul lives in God for the most part, needs the corresponding programs of behavior, speech and work for the earthly existence. This combination of programs allows the person to live in the world and enables him to deal with all that comes toward him each day. However, to live in the world, does not mean to be with the world, with its customs and excesses.

In my soul, I grasp all the details of the eternal truth, which cannot be expressed with our human vocabulary. What I receive from the eternal Spirit, God, that is, what is addressed in me by the Spirit's impulses of light, I likewise behold in my innermost being and recognize with certainty that it is as I see it before me in my innermost being.

The experiencing and understanding of all things very gradually opened up in me, as the soul became one with the great, mighty, eternal Spirit, with the All and the All-One. I know and do not doubt for a moment that it is as I perceive it in me. I know it is the truth, but I cannot prove it. I do not have to, nor do I want to, prove it.

Anyone who feels secure in God knows that God directs all things and that one day the truth will be evident in ever more people. The words about the truth are shells; this is why the word is merely the reflection of the core, of the truth. We are all heirs to infinity, and that is where the path leads to, which each soul will take one day. One day, to each maturing soul the consciousness which makes us divine will be manifest. Then the ensouled human being will experience and grasp what the unknowing ones dismiss as the "mysteries of God."

It is as it is: God *is*, and the being in Him is divine. The being, the soul, is not separate from the origin of the wellspring and from the wellspring itself. It is always in the source and is the source itself. It is symphony and harmony – it is light and unity with all Being: It is in God.

The truth that speaks from the soul through me, the human being, is spoken for all who want to find God in their innermost being and immerse in the life, in the source – for we are children of God.

Again and again, I have to mention that the fight comes before the victory. Until I had reached the inner goal, the hardest struggles were necessary. Only through the continual struggle with the all-too-human, base ego, did the human being, out of love for God, bow before the almighty I Am, and the soul immersed in the law of life, in the I Am, in God.

My soul grew in the fight against the base ego and was strengthened through the victory over myself, the human being. Like the Phoenix rises out of the ashes, so did the soul grow out of the base self through the person's struggle, privation and self-denial. In the fight with myself, I gained ever more love for God and from the love for God, the love for my neighbor.

Anyone who wants to be victorious over himself is given the strength. He already bears the victory in himself. The one who merely talks about struggle loses the struggle and remains who he is – the person who speaks only of himself.

Again and again, I am asked: "How did you manage it?" – And again and again, I have to say: I struggled. At first, I struggled for the knowledge that God exists, then, for the love for God, so as to discard my faults and weaknesses.

What do all these many words mean? No one can convince another. But I want to bear witness to the One who has won me, to the One I let win me: to God in whom my soul is. Everything that I say about myself should merely be impulses for all those who set out on the way to God or who are on the way to God.

The one who has reached the origin of the wellspring will no longer talk about himself, the human being. God speaks through him and the person beholds what God reveals to him, because the word of life, the light, which radiates through the divine beings of the heavens and the purified souls, is heaven itself.

If the philosopher's stone, God, shines in the person's soul, then words seem dark and meaningless to him, because the light of God shows him all that the word cannot express.

Nevertheless, the word of God, the eternal truth, is set in the vessel of words of the human language; it is a precious good for those who long for the eternal truth. The one who learns to grasp and understand the meaning of the word and lives what he learns from the word grows closer to the divine. His soul immerses ever more in the stream of Being. In this way, it reaches the source and lives in the origin of the source, which is eternal revelation and eternal perception.

Through the guidance of the Eternal and His immediate proximity, I have learned and experienced what it means to selflessly accept and receive my neighbor, without differences. Even when many a one is not well-disposed toward me, I have learned to keep him in my heart.

A Proponent of the Eternal Truth, of the Law of Life, Is Not Always Comfortable for His Fellow People

An autobiography not only touches upon the occurrences and events. It goes into depth particularly where it personally concerns the author. The title of this book is: *A Woman's Life in Service of the Eternal.* It was and is in fact a woman's life in service of the Eternal. This life was and is, from the perspective of the human being, loneliness, steadfastness in God, self-forgetfulness and hard work. A life – ultimately lonely in God. God showed and revealed the heavens to me. He also revealed it to my fellow people. But many made me go through hell.

People can live among people and yet are alone, above all when they strive toward the Eternal. That's how it was for me. To me applies solely the law of life, God, the infinite love. That is my life. Because I know that God is love and thus, a Father of love, I remain steadfast in this awareness, even when people want to impose their theories or all-too-human willing on me.

A proponent of the eternal truth is not always comfortable for her fellow people, quite the contrary. She is frequently avoided and treated with hostility, because she clearly, that is, forthrightly, speaks the truth and places her finger on the wound of the all-too-human ego. This is how it was from the beginning of the Homebringing Mission and this is also how it is today, for I do not depend on human opinions. I live and follow solely the eternal Spirit, whose instrument I am. Since God is freedom, I leave to each person the freedom to think and live as he wishes.

I was and am for justice. This is why, since the beginning of the prophetic word, I have done everything to surrender my all-too-human ego to the One who can transform it into divine selflessness. In manifold ways and means, I had to experience and overcome myself, until I learned to hold up with Christ.

Right from the beginning, since the Eternal called to life the work of the Christ of God, I strive for it not to become an institution. An institution is not founded on the principles of equality, freedom, unity, brotherliness and justice. It is structured hierarchically, and instead of equality, a graduated subjection to directives exists in an institution, which bears the lack of freedom in itself. Thus, neither freedom nor voluntariness exist; and so, true unity and brotherliness cannot grow. Unity and brotherliness can develop only when the individual is no longer concerned about himself, his advancement and his well-being, but about the well-being of all, the common good.

A Woman's Life in Service of the Eternal – a mission, in which I, as we say, "held my own" day after day, which means I had, and have, to deploy all the powers available to me. If these were merely the powers of the human being, of the woman, then the great achievements would not have developed; but it was, and is, the Spirit of God, of the Almighty, who worked, and works, through me. I was, and am, constantly aware that I am in service of God, and my human being also uncompromisingly bowed to the will of the Eternal after the initial resistance of which I have already reported.

The woman did not let herself be impressed by either money and property, or masculinity and male courtship. I remained, and remain, what the Lord expected of me: His instrument and His emissary in the mighty work of the Eternal, a woman in service of the selfless, impersonal love.

The Church Institution Broke into Our Family Life with Intrigues and Defamations

When the church institutions broke into our family life with intrigues and defamations, what Jesus of Nazareth said came true to me: *If they have persecuted me, they will also persecute you.*

And: *Whoever loves husband, wife or child more than me is not worthy of me.* I gave my yes to the Eternal. What else could I do but what many other prophets did before me: keep the yes and continue the Lord's mission.

It was made indirectly clear to me to leave the house that had provided me with a home and earthly secureness. What else could I do but go? With a few personal items, such as money, clothing and an old car, the prophet had to leave the security of her home. As usual with all callings of a true prophet of God: God, the Eternal, fetches the human being in the prophetic mission from hearth and home and places him in this service.

God helped. During the low times, He let me sense and experience what it means: "Lord, I will not leave You, for You bless me." He blessed me and helped me to take these hurdles. He also helped me to draw lessons from them for the spiritual teaching. And He helped me to gain understanding for my fellow people from this hardship. He lifted me up and placed me in His service again. The human being in bondage and the purified soul rose like the Phoenix from the ashes, and the woman, whom God calls His prophetess, grew steadfast in Him, and against all further adversities that I had, and have, to endure from pastors, priests, church commissioners and their followers.

   I have now been serving the Eternal for many years, and my soul is in Him, the mighty stream of life. I am not in this world to be with this world. I came into this world with brothers and sisters to serve our Brother and Redeemer, Christ, and to rehabilitate Him, whose name has been, and still is, defamed, scorned, mocked and discriminated against for nearly two thousand years. His name was, and is, abused in honor of the human ego, primarily in the church institutions.
   Christ is the guardian of the truth and, out of grace and in thankfulness, I may be His instrument.

Lonely Among People

Besides all these initial difficulties in building the divine work, came the ever stronger attacks by those commissioned by the church institutions to fight against religious minorities. So I was constantly under crossfire. Adversities, defamations, scorn and mockery came from all directions.

Slander was also added by those who could not push through their own personal inclinations in the work of God, that is, who could not crown their habitus, their ego, at the cost of the Christ of God.

To be able to bear up against all this, you may not think of yourself, nor look at yourself as a person, but must deny yourself and rely solely on Christ, so as to clear the jungle that others have sown, or wanted to sow, with their human ego. In many situations, I had to walk the path through this undergrowth of the all-too-human ego alone, and frequently had to clear it alone as well.

These efforts, to clear the path through the jungle of the all-too-humanness, made me lonely. On this path, I had no one at my side with whom I could have spoken about my heartache.

About the many inconsistencies that my fellow people burdened my heart with, I could talk only with the eternal Father, with Christ and with Brother Emanuel, because no one understood me. Many around me had, as already mentioned, their own ideas and theories, which were inacceptable to me because they were not in accordance with the eternal law. Through this, I grew lonely in the external world. I often made attempts to exchange views with someone, for I was and am a human being. But over and over again, I had to recognize that when I went to my neighbor with what was making my heart heavy, I rarely found understanding. A brother or sister seldom responded to the pain in my heart. I could share my experiences, my agitations, my suffering and loneliness with no one.

Through the external isolation and the absolute devotion to the Spirit of God, and based on the spiritual-divine expansion of consciousness, an ever greater distance between the all-too-human aspects of my fellow people and me developed. As a human being, I often found this very painful.

The prophet is usually misunderstood. Many are of the opinion that the prophet is a person who feels and thinks like themselves. The reason for this is that the true prophet joins the ranks of his brothers and sisters and is thus seen as a mere human being. But the inner life of the prophet is totally different. All his thoughts and aspirations are to fulfill the will of God and to bring God's love and wisdom into this world. During the past years, that has been my sole concern, and it still is even today. It is my life. The basic vibration of the prophet is always God.

From Early in the Morning Until Late – I Am Always There, Responsibly

Now (1997) I have passed my 64th year of life. However, my workload has not dimished, on the contrary. In terms of the teaching activity within the world-spanning work of God and the spiritual literature, I am monumentally occupied, for example, from early in the morning until late in the evening, and that, nearly every day. I work with others in all the spiritual spheres of the work that has become worldwide.

Whether it is the Inner Path, which, among other things, is also prepared and commented on for radio programs, whether it is the roundtable discussions that are part of the transmissions of the Inner Path, whether it is the teaching activity in the Cosmic School of Life, and much more – I am always there, responsibly.

So there is seldom a free evening and a free weekend, seldom a free morning or afternoon. Even if, for once, I plan to allow myself a free day – obligations call again and again.

The Spirit of the Christ of God makes use of the free hours, so to speak, and places more spiritual-divine principles of the law into my awareness, which promote and enlarge His work, so that it increases in light and power more and more.

In discussions and schoolings, I then pass on these divine aspects to those brothers and sisters who have the corresponding abilities, expert knowledge and experiences to transfer them with me into matter. Thus, the prophet is assiduously active.

Christ is the Lord of His work, who lets His power flow abundantly. Those who are active in His work bear the responsibility to see that the divine water of life is applied in the right way.

Through God's love and grace I may draw from the immediate eternal wellspring and give the highest from the primordial source, to the extent that it can be expressed with human words.
By way of my spiritual consciousness, which opens more and more, the Spirit of the Christ of God continued to expand and build His divine work and made it worldwide. Consciously or unconsciously, all souls and ultimately, all human beings have the same goal, to receive peace and love.

God is unity. The different degrees of consciousness of the people are not a separation from the unity, because God eternally bears His children in His unity, in His heart.

For the Reader

This autobiography, which lays bare a part of my life, is the truth. I am not the one who made me a prophet, but rather God called me to this. I am a human being and sister among brothers and sisters. That is my life and my concern, that all people see me this way. God speaks of His prophetess, but not your sister Gabriele.

Dear brothers, dear sisters, who have read this autobiography, let me be among you as a sister. For as it is in heaven, so shall it be on Earth. No matter what task or what divine mission we have, we are brothers and sisters in heaven and on Earth. That is what I am and that is what I will remain, on Earth and in eternity.

Your sister
Gabriele

The Workings of Gabriele, the Divine Wisdom
– Sophia –
in the Earthly Garment

*For as the rain
and the snow come down from heaven
and do not return there
but water the earth,
making it bring forth and sprout,
giving seed to the sower
and bread to the eater,
so shall my word be
that goes out from my mouth;
it shall not return to me empty,
but it shall accomplish that
which I purpose,
and shall succeed
in the thing for which I sent it.*

(Isaiah 55:10-11)

Dear fellow people,

following the autobiography that Gabriele wrote in 1997, in which she, in all modesty and humility, shares with us her life as a woman in service of the Eternal, her contemporaries report about the workings of Gabriele, the great prophetess of God, through whom the Christ of God prepares His return in the Spirit.

In her autobiographical descriptions, Gabriele gives us such vivid insight into her development as a human being and her calling to be the prophetess of God that we don't want to overlay it with too many detailed accounts of her decades-long and manifold work for the Kingdom of God.

Every description of her work – be it ever so extensive – would always provide only a small reflection of what the Eternal in reality created, and creates, through the divine Wisdom, Sophia.

The work of the deed of the love for God and neighbor is therefore passed on here only in a brief overview, a brief look into the superhuman achievement and significant creative power that Gabriele brought in her life as a woman for the Kingdom of God, for her fellow human beings, for all souls, yes, for God's creation, and still brings until today.

The divine Wisdom, Sophia, was effective in all generations, in putting into practice what the Wisdom teaches.

This is also the case again now in this mighty time of radical change. The Love and the Wisdom created and accomplishes, so that what was announced will be: The New Jerusalem, the basis for the Kingdom of Peace of Jesus Christ.

What was essentially said to Gabriele from the Kingdom of God at the beginning of the prophetic word – *What the Eternal and His Son, Christ, want is that a worldwide work be built up through you* – has taken place. The work of the Christ of God is worldwide.

Gabriele – Sophia, the divine Wisdom – created and accomplishes the basis for the New Jerusalem.
The foundations have been laid. From the Kingdom of God resounds the call: *We lay out and build up.*

Gabriele, the Emissary of God, Travelled to Many Countries of the Earth on Behalf of the Eternal

Soon after the beginning of the prophetic activity, in the years from 1979 until the end of the 1980s, Gabriele began to travel to various cities in all the German-speaking region, often several times in a week, to give the divine word of revelation to the people.

Following the desire of the Eternal and of His Son, Christ – to build a worldwide work – during the years from 1981 to 1986, Gabriele undertook many long trips abroad, to carry His word into all the world.

For this, Gabriele travelled to Italy, Spain, France, Finland and other European countries as well as overseas to Canada, Mexico and the USA. During the same time that she was making approximately 60 trips abroad in only five years, she wrote numerous pamphlets and books, taught the Inner Path to the Cosmic Consciousness, gave divine revelations in the then developing Inner Spirit=Christ Churches and explained the spiritual principles of the Kingdom of God.

Already during these years, Christ called willing people to create with Him the basis for a new era, the era of the Christ of God, in which a new humanity of higher ethics and morals should be lived.

Out of love for Him, the Eternal, she, a sensitive, reserved and delicate woman, stepped before the people – also aware that she might be mocked and scorned. And she had to bitterly experience what it means to be rejected, despised and reviled on account of the word of God, above all, by the representatives of the institutional mainstream churches.

During the many trips abroad, divine revelations were given through Gabriele in various cities within just a few days. This always meant strenuous journeys through the respective country and contact with people who wanted to become responsible for the work of the Christ of God in the individual countries and had endlessly many questions for Gabriele.

People's interest varied widely: Sometimes only a few people came to the divine revelations – but often it was over a thousand people, so that there wasn't enough room in the rented halls.

The Spirit of God explained that, at the beginning, sometimes fewer people would come because the atmosphere of the respective city or country first has to be prepared. And that is what happened. In all the cities and countries where Gabriele travelled back then, divine revelations and the teachings of the Free Spirit can be received today via many radio and television stations.

The list of cities where great revelations of the Spirit of the Christ of God were given is manifold and incomplete:

Guadalajara in Mexico; Chicago, Denver, Colorado Springs, New York, Philadelphia, Cleveland, New Haven, Phoenicia, Westport und Boston in the USA, and Toronto in Canada. And in Europe: Turin, Milano, Florence, Rome and Salice Terme in Italy; then Madrid, Barcelona, Malaga and Seville in Spain; Melilla in North Africa; Strasbourg, Nancy, Lyon, Marseille, Paris in France and Helsinki in Finland. Gabriele traveled to many cities several times, to give revelations from the Christ of God.

When Gabriele returned from one of these strenuous trips abroad, things continued without pause. Parallel to the long trips abroad, the Spirit of the Christ of God also continued to give revelations in many cities in Germany, Austria and Switzerland. Gabriele also led seminars and schoolings for spiritually seeking people in various cities. On the one hand, she wrote in books and pamphlets what God, the Eternal, and Christ revealed to her, and on the other hand, she drew from her opened consciousness, producing numerous works on all spheres of life. Meanwhile, many of the far more than 100 books and pamphlets with teachings from the Kingdom of God have been translated into many different languages, including various regional African languages, and are thus available to people all over the world.

In addition, the message of the Free Spirit is broadcast via radio and television stations around the globe.

Divine revelations, schoolings of the Inner Path to the Cosmic Consciousness, programs for nature and the animals, roundtable discussions, for example, about reincarnation as a component of early Christian belief or about life after death; "Spiritual Help for the Day" and "Original Christian Meditations" – just to mention a few examples – an be received by millions of radio listeners and television viewers worldwide.

Today, God's message is passed on by way of approximately 550 radio stations in 56 countries and over 850 television stations in 65 countries.

In addition, there are the following television stations: *Gabriele TV Africa*, which broadcasts over the African continent, *Sophia TV America*, which can be received in North, South and Central America, and in Europe, stations such as *Sophia TV, Die Neue Zeit TV, Sender New Jerusalem* and many other regional stations. There are also several Internet radio and television channels.

The Beginning of New Jerusalem

Already in the 1980s, through the divine Wisdom, the Christ of God called people from all four winds, to establish with Him the foundations for the emergent Kingdom of Peace of Jesus Christ.

Many who are in the mission of God followed the call of the Christ of God and came together to create the basis for the New Jerusalem.

Together, they founded the Covenant Community New Jerusalem, the beginning of the central light for the emergent Kingdom of Peace of Jesus Christ.

But many sons and daughters of God let themselves be ensnared by sin. They loved the sin, and put the work of the deed of love and wisdom in second place. They again laid down what they had promised the Eternal and His Son, Christ, and their fellow human beings.

Despite all this, Gabriele – Sophia, the divine Wisdom – created and accomplished, thus laying the basis for what shall become: the foundation for the New Jerusalem.

She created and accomplished – and enterprises emerged, which were to be developed and led in the Spirit of the Christ of God – Christ-enterprises.

She created and accomplished – and a Christ-clinic emerged.

She created and accomplished – and a Christ-school in Universal Life came into being as well as kindergartens.

She created and accomplished – and social service providers and homes for the elderly came into being.

She created and accomplished – and several agricultural enterprises were founded. They work according to the concept from the Spirit of God "from cultivation to the customer."

She created and accomplished – and artisan enterprises came into being, small units for all spheres of life that work hand in hand with each other.

Vegetarian gastronomy firms emerged – restaurants and cafés as well as service firms.

She created and accomplished – and the *Sophia Spessart Houses* came into being, guest houses, among other things, for people who want to get to know the work of the Christ of God.

For all these spheres and branches of business, Gabriele gave schoolings over many years, week after week, schoolings on the concept of operation according to the Sermon on the Mount of Jesus of Nazareth, in order to provide a spiritual basis for an emerging people in the Spirit of the Christ of God.

Looking back on this time, the Christ of God spoke in *This Is My Word. Alpha and Omega. The Gospel of Jesus*, to the people in the future Kingdom of Peace:

To be able to fulfill the laws of God in all areas of life, they set up artisan enterprises and acquired farms. They founded kindergartens, father-mother-houses, schools, clinics and homes for the elderly. They thus began building up everything that people needed for the New Era and in the New Era. They placed all the new and developing activities for the Kingdom of God into the law of God which reads: Pray and work, and keep peace with your neighbor. …

The prophetess and emissary of God stood in the midst of this time of setting out and of radical change. She was loved and respected by some people and despised, doubted, slandered and ridiculed by others. As in My time as Jesus of Nazareth, the Pharisees and scribes again incited the people against Me, the Universal Spirit, so as to silence Me. To no avail! They passed away – and the New Era, the Kingdom of Peace of Jesus Christ, emerged. (pp. 418-19)

Gabriele – Sophia, the divine Wisdom – unceasingly taught, and teaches, the Inner Path to the Cosmic Consciousness, so that we human beings find our way to God in us.

She taught people in the following of Jesus of Nazareth, in order to build up a people of the Spirit with higher ethics and morals, which lives according to the five principles: equality, freedom, unity and brotherliness, from which follows justice.

She created the *Worldwide Center of the Christ of God for Prayer and Healing by Faith*, which is the hope and support for many people all over the world who suffer illness and hardship.

She initiated and founded the Land of Peace, the land of Love and Wisdom, under the sign of the Lily.

In the year 2000, Gabriele founded the *International Gabriele Foundations, the Saamlinic Work*.

With this, she laid the foundation for the Kingdom of Peace of Jesus Christ, which God had announced through His great prophet Isaiah already 2700 years ago. God, the Eternal, spoke:

The wolf shall dwell with the lamb, and the leopard shall lie down with the young goat, and the calf and the lion ... together; and a little child shall lead them. The cow and the bear shall graze; their young shall lie down together; and the lion shall eat straw like the ox. The nursing child shall play over the hole of the cobra, and the weaned child shall put his hand on the adder's den.

They shall not hurt or destroy in all my holy mountain; for the earth shall be full of the knowledge of the Lord as the waters cover the sea. (Isaiah 11:6-9)

Today, the words of the prophet of God, Isaiah, in whom the Cherub of divine Wisdom was incarnated, are being fulfilled through the Seraph of divine Wisdom in the earthly garment, Gabriele. And what God, the Eternal, spoke through Isaiah is being fulfilled:

*… so shall my word be
that goes out from my mouth;
it shall not return to me empty,
but it shall accomplish that which
I purpose, and shall succeed in the
thing for which I sent it.*

Gabriele – Sophia, the divine Wisdom – created and accomplished *the International Gabriele Foundations in Africa* according to the role model of the mother foundation in Germany.

Many people in Africa who have gotten to know God's word through Gabriele, came together under the promise of Jesus of Nazareth, the Christ of God:

Wherever two or three are gathered in My name, I am there in the midst of them. They formed original communities and have very active exchanges with the mother foundation in Germany, which supports them. They founded Sophia Schools and care for orphaned children and needy persons.

Gabriele – Sophia, the divine Wisdom – created and accomplished the groundwork for beautiful housing, embedded in park-like residential areas.

The harmonious, primarily rounded building forms with bowfronts, little towers and imaginative ground plans, whose forms are derived from nature, were received by Gabriele in the inner vision from the Kingdom of God; she implemented them into the possibilities of the three dimensions, for the beginning of the New Jerusalem.

Anyone who wants to get to know the work and activity of Gabriele in all its fullness is warmly invited to visit the *Sophia Library* and inform him- or herself in detail.

The design of the *Sophia Library* itself gives us a sense of what wealth of ideas Gabriele is able to draw from. In only six weeks, hand in hand with a team of enthusiastic artisans, she transformed a formerly simple, rectangular room into a multifaceted library, where events and concerts also take place.

And Gabriele – Sophia, the divine Wisdom – created more:
The Tent of God among the People for All the Nations of this Earth, under the Sign of the Lily, the Ark of the Covenant of the Free Spirit – New Jerusalem.

The tent of God among the people is not being built for Original Christians alone.
The Tent of God Among the People for All the Nations of this Earth, under the Sign of the Lily, Sophia, the Ark of the Covenant of the Free Spirit – New Jerusalem, will become a symbol for all people in all nations, who worship the Spirit of the Christ of God, and walk the path of the primordial Wisdom, of Sophia, the divine Wisdom.

In all the generations of this world, God's primordial Wisdom entered the consciousness of many people who honor the Eternal One.
Over the generations, Sophia, the Wisdom, went over the Earth in female form and brought to the people the Wisdom of God, the primordial light of the Being, in spoken and written form.
Today, the time has come in which the Eternal One has presented to Sophia, to the divine Wisdom – the divine

male principle in the Kingdom of God and the female principle in Gabriele – the lily, which she passes on to all seeking people in love and consolation, in awareness of the words of Jesus of Nazareth: *I come soon.*

The appearance of the light of the Christ of God and His being of love, gentleness and kindness will – after the battle of the nations – call and lead together the still existing peoples to a nation of the life.

For the return of Sophia to the Father's house, *The Tent of God Among the People for All the Nations of this Earth, under the Sign of the Lily, the Ark of the Covenant of the Free Spirit – New Jerusalem* stands as a symbol and, at the same time, Christ and the divine Wisdom stand, in the Spirit, for the instructions from the eternal Being.

The Illusion "I Know Her" –
Contemporary Witnesses Report

To completely comprehend a person is hardly possible for anyone. Why? Because only the person who has fathomed himself can look into the depths of his neighbor. Who has ever recognized himself in the depths of his being? That is why it is always a very limited undertaking when a person wants to describe another. This is all the more true when the person wants to explain or describe the nature and consciousness of a person with a higher consciousness. So every description of Gabriele will always merely point out aspects that find their limit in the author's capacity to perceive. Therefore: "The illusion – I know her."

It is not at all possible to completely grasp Gabriele as the prophetess of God and as the incarnated Seraph of the divine Wisdom and put this into words, since the author's words, as well as the reader's terminology, are shaped by their respective consciousness.

For this reason, the great emissaries of love from the Kingdom of God have gone, and go, over this world largely unrecognized and misunderstood.

If, like the great prophets of God, they have to proclaim their true nature to humankind, so that they can be effective as guides toward the Kingdom of God, then for the prophets in human form this is surely the most difficult part of their service to God and the people.

Thus, Jesus of Nazareth Himself had to state that He is the Son of God. It was revealed to the Christ of God in Jesus of Nazareth and He Himself had to say: *See, one greater than Moses is here.* Or: *The Father and I are one* and *The one who has seen me has seen the Father.*

Words, which outraged His contemporaries – prejudiced in their dogmatic thinking by the ritual leaders of their religion – and led to the diabolic plan to kill Jesus, the Christ, to do away with Him and wipe out His teachings.

As the human being Jesus of Nazareth, He had to state Himself that He is the promised Messiah. He had to state Himself that He will come again in the Comforter, the Spirit of truth, who leads us human beings into all the truth.

To fulfill this promise, the Eternal sent His Seraph of divine Wisdom from the Sanctum, from the Kingdom of God, the female principle of His primordial Wisdom, who is in His Father-heart as present Being since the primordial beginning of creation.

Her being is inextricably linked in the duality with the law-prince before the throne of God, the Cherub of divine Wisdom.

The Seraph of divine Wisdom incarnated into a human child, a girl, who grew up without knowing about this all-encompassing mission, as Gabriele explains in her autobiography.

In 1975, when Gabriele was informed about her mission for the Kingdom of God at the age of 42, it was a profound turning point in her life.

It was explained to Gabriele who she is as a spirit being and which heavenly being, as her dual, is her spiritual teacher, in order to prepare and train her as the instrument of the Christ of God, as the prophetess of the Eternal. For the Earth, the being before God's throne was introduced to her as Emanuel, who, on behalf of the Almighty, accompanies her as her teacher on the way to the prophetic activity. But he, who introduced himself with the plain name of Brother Emanuel, is the law-prince of the third basic power of God and is inextricably linked with Gabriele, the Seraph of divine Wisdom.

Since then, the Infinite, the Christ of God, in unity with the heavenly prince-pair of the divine Wisdom – the Cherub in the spirit and the Seraph, Gabriele, in the earthly garment – has been unceasingly creating and working for the Kingdom of God on this Earth, so that today the call of the Eternal rings out: the onset of the Messianic and Sophianic Age Under the Sign of the Lily.

A Contemporary Witness

I've known Gabriele, the prophetess and emissary of God, since the beginning of the 1990s.

The first time I heard Gabriele as God's teaching prophetess was in the Inner Spirit=Christ Church in Basel, Switzerland.

Back then, many people were connected all over Europe via teleconference and could directly take part in the discussion on the teaching contemplations. Gabriele taught about *The Great Cosmic Teachings of Jesus of Nazareth to His Disciples and Apostles, Who Could Understand Them*, which the Spirit of the Christ of God had revealed through her in the prophetic word.

Every Friday evening, she explained the Christ-revelation and interpreted His word in a depth and multifaceted way that was simply overwhelming to me. In my heart, I felt that the divine Wisdom was directly working here, because in each word, in each sentence and even in each answer that Gabriele gave a listener, lay the fullness of the divine Wisdom. And it became a certainty to me that here is the word of truth that Jesus of Nazareth had spoken about:

I will send you the Comforter, the Spirit of truth, who will lead you into all the truth.

As it turned out, I must not have fooled myself. Until this very day, I am privileged to experience how Gabriele works for the eternal truth from the Kingdom of God. She gives the word with the full authority of the Spirit of the Christ of God and of the Eternal, All-One, God.

The prophet of God spoke about the Free Spirit, about the All-Law – yes, God Himself and the Christ of God spoke through this person precisely about this inner freedom that I had always sought.

Above all, the alternative to external religions was pointed out: the path to within, the path to the expansion of consciousness, the path into the inner freedom, the becoming free of one's own burdens, in order to draw closer to God in one's own inner being, independent of external human leadership.

The question preoccupied me: Who is this woman who, so filled with simplicity, grace and with a winning warmth, represents this authority of the Spirit? I pricked up my ears when I learned that the Seraph of divine Wisdom is incarnated in her and that she works directly in connection with the Cherub of divine Wisdom, the law-angel before the throne of God.

It was only little by little that I could sense who lives among us. Always when I thought I had grasped it, I had to soon realize that I had come to know mere facets of her true nature, which made me believe that I had now completely recognized who lives among us in Gabriele. That's how it is until today.

To have the privilege of participating in teaching contemplations with Gabriele, and listen to her divine schoolings, in which every single word, so dynamic and fresh, so true to life, falls directly into the heart, was an uplifting feeling back then as today.

Just as it was said of Jesus of Nazareth: *and He led them onto a mountain,* so I felt each time as if carried onto the heights, from which perspective I could grasp many a thing in my life and about the eternal Being that until then had been closed to me. Something strange was happening to me, because I may have been a seeker, but I had, nevertheless, established my life in the world. Thus, quite a bit rebelled in me against the new insights, because I sensed that they would turn my life inside out. A life oriented to the external world is not at all in accord with the Sermon on the Mount of Jesus of Nazareth.

And yet, as often as I heard Gabriele's voice and could experience the Wisdom that she lived, I felt addressed in my inner being and the realization grew in me:

Here you cannot remain a mere listener of the word, here you are being asked to help and build with others, what was, and is, brought to us people with great hope and certainty from the Kingdom of God: the building of the New Jerusalem for the Kingdom of Peace of Jesus Christ.

A short time later, I got to know Gabriele in seminars, where, with a few questions, she gave me incredible help for my life, which, to some extent, I had to work on for some time, so that I could put into practice what I became aware of through her questions and explanations. Through this, I was privileged to learn that through her opened consciousness, Gabriele grasps each person in his depths and knows exactly what word, which question or impulse will help her neighbor further.

With all that I could learn on the Inner Path, the call in me to work with others became louder, to be active for the work of the Christ of God.

It was not without struggles and difficulties that I broke camp, as it were, back then, and cleared private and professional relationships, so that I could be free for new tasks in the work of the Christ of God in the vicinity of Würzburg.

With all this, I learned to understand more and more from what humility and love for God Gabriele attained the capacity to endure that enabled her to bear all the adverse circumstances that were caused to her by people servile to the church or working in the media, but also by those fellow people who may have given their yes to the Christ of God, but then acted to the contrary.

In many conversations, Gabriele speaks very openly about how much grief all these ugly and in part vile characters of her fellow people have caused her, and to a certain extent still do until today.

With this, I learned to understand that in everything that she does for God, the Eternal, Gabriele's steadfastness, her single-mindedness and willingness to sacrifice her divine Wisdom and self-possession cannot hide the fact that as a woman she endured all these unprincipled low blows of her fellow people thanks only to her unshakable love for God, having gained her capacity to endure in countless, deeply bitter hours of anguish and suffering.

As sisterly close and mild as Gabriele is, she can be just as decisive, straightforward and unbending when the work of the Christ of God is endangered by wrongdoings of individuals. Particularly when, through their dominant program world, male companions wanted, or want, to reshape the work of the Christ of God into their vehicle, with her spiritual authority, she protects the work of the Christ of God from such patriarchic influences.
In this, she possesses an incredible, mental strategic ability, with which she prevents the influence of institutional machinations in every case. The delicate, fine woman stood, and stands, heroically before the work of the Christ of God and until today, defies anyone who prepares to turn the work of the Christ of God into an institution.

Her Life in a Foreign Land

Gabriele is a person of the Spirit through and through.

Thereby, she is true to life and does not like sentimental, effusive behavior at all.

As a spiritually self-possessed person, she knows the requirements of life on Earth and takes care of them as long as it is important for the life on Earth of the being from the eternal homeland.

She also tackles very practically everything that concerns dealing with daily life. She helps and gives tips on how much of what daily life brings with it can be dealt with more easily.

Her down-to-earth manner is refreshing and does one good, and her great sense of fellowship could tempt one to believe that she experiences the situations, conversations and events as we perceive them. Many are fooled by this illusion.

Gabriele's true nature, her spiritual nature, is not of this world. With her, one can learn what it means to live in the world, but not with the world. However, what this means for a sensitive person can only be surmised.

Over and over again, we are witnesses of the fact that Gabriele hears what others do not hear; she sees what others do not see; she feels what others do not feel. In her inner world, she lives in dialogue with the Kingdom of God, whose emissary she is.

And yet, we also experience that it is a heavy burden for her to live as a human being among human beings who have hardly any access to their true being. Because of this, even in the midst of her fellow people, Gabriele's life on Earth is mostly a permanent life in a foreign land.

Even though Gabriele hardly lets it show, it can be sensed that her life in foreign parts is especially hard to bear when her fellow people, who said yes to the great Spirit of life, God, the Eternal, then turned their back on Him, because their world of desires and ideas had not been fulfilled.

Even though Gabriele knows about the deeper-lying causes and the context of the behavior of her fellow people, it is, however, incomprehensible to her, because of her own steadfast loyalty to the spiritual homeland, when people who have given a free yes to God, the Eternal, to a life in the Spirit of God, again seek out the world to fulfill their egocentric life of desires.

She is shocked when people cling so much to their wrong attitudes, which, however, only cause them worries and hardship, when they don't clear up the hostility with their neighbor, in order to go forward toward the great goal, to establish a Kingdom of Peace that is not utopia, but will become reality, when people set out to walk in the footsteps of Jesus of Nazareth.

Great Moments

Special great moments are when Gabriele speaks about the events of creation, about the make-up of the pure Being, the infinite spiritual solar systems: how they were beheld and created by the Eternal, how they are designed and how they continue to develop in the unceasing evolution of the Kingdom of God.

Or when Gabriele speaks about the Son of God and the mighty event of redemption for creation, and her whole love and devotion for the Christ of God can be sensed in each word.

During these hours, you feel very close to heaven – and yet you have to conclude that Gabriele is not only closer to heaven, she is a part of heaven, of the Kingdom of God, in full consciousness, linked through and through with Christ, with God-Father and with the law-princes of the Kingdom of God.

The deep insights into the spiritual processes of creation that she conveys to us are limited only by the possibilities of our language, which always has to resort to the pictures and descriptions from the three dimensions to convey to us human beings a touch of the mighty workings of the Eternal in the infinite course of creation.

Gabriele also explained to us why she can describe the events of creation, the make-up of the pure Being, the becoming and working of God:

In her innermost being, she knows about all things through the duality with the Cherub of divine Wisdom, the law-prince before the throne of God, who from the very beginning was present at creation. From this source of primordial Wisdom, Gabriele can draw as much as human words are able to express at all.

Gabriele herself terms the explanations and descriptions of the heavenly Being as "a small look through a crack in the door," and through her words, which are filled with great devotion and love for the Kingdom of God, you sense that in her inner being she grasps much, much more than she can convey to us. Gabriele hears and knows; she sees and knows, yet the language of our earthly existence is limited, and moreover, the absorption capacity of us listeners is respectively shaped by our own consciousness and our own concepts.

As God's emissary, Gabriele conveys the message of the Kingdom of God into our forbidding, foreign world, which is marked by the one against the other, by fighting and hostility. In this enemy territory, as the emissary of God, she has to hold the line for her homeland, the Kingdom of God, with which she is unceasingly connected and whose message of love for God and neighbor she conveys. In all things she represents her spiritual homeland through and through, so as to work on the Earth, in a foreign land, for the return of the souls and human beings who once left the homeland, the Kingdom of God.

Gabriele's descriptions of the Kingdom of God are far from every kind of sentimentality. All church-adhered "Hallelujah" posturing about the Kingdom of God is repugnant to her. For her, the Kingdom of God, the eternal, pure Being, is a reality that can be experienced.

In reverence and great humility, she tells of the make-up of the Kingdom of God, of the cradle of drawing and creating, in which God's creation-children grow up.

Dialogue with God

After over 40 years of prophetic activity, many people worldwide know Gabriele as the prophetess and emissary of God. The Christ of God speaks through her. She schools as the teaching prophetess of God.

But what additionally distinguishes her in her very special relationship to God, our Father, to Christ, the Son of the Eternal, and to the Cherub of divine Wisdom, for us human beings called Brother Emanuel, is Gabriele's direct dialogue with the highest beings of the Kingdom of God. She speaks with God, with Christ and with the law-prince of the divine Wisdom – and they answer her. She asks and receives an answer.

She often shares these dialogues with us, telling about the conversations with God, with Christ or with her dual, the Cherub of divine Wisdom.

In her dialogue with the Eternal, God does not speak through the prophetic word via Gabriele, but as a Father to His daughter. In this dialogue, she is totally a daughter to the Eternal, her Father, and totally a sister to us brothers and sisters. As the questioner, she, who in her inner being knows about everything, is totally a pupil and lines up in humility before the great Spirit of the All, as a sister among her brothers and sisters.

What Gabriele takes for granted – that God, the Eternal, Christ and the Cherub of divine Wisdom, Brother Emanuel, speak to and with her – is, for those who may be present during these special moments when the Father or His Son, Christ, speak to a few brothers and sisters, an especially uplifting experience.

Particularly in the direct experience of Gabriele's humility, in her devotion to the great Creator-God, in how she integrates herself into a group of brothers and sisters, lies the greatness of the true prophet of God. It is these special moments for those present, which can hardly be expressed in words. Through this modest human child, Gabriele, heaven opens up in these moments and speaks the word of the heavens into the souls of those present. The near God can be sensed through and through. He reveals Himself in the clear word, which is always love. And when the words are sometimes earnest, admonishing or warning, in their origin, they are always love – love for His children, love for His creation, love and fatherly care, and the call for the return home of all His children.

Because of their duality, Gabriele is especially deeply linked with the Cherub of divine Wisdom, the law prince before God's throne, simply called Brother Emanuel on Earth, for they are two and yet one, infinitely and eternally linked with one another in working for the Kingdom of God.

He is her spiritual teacher, who prepared her for the prophetic office, and during the years of training in the earthly garment, she was his pupil. Still today, she can ask him about anything and he gives the answer from the law of God. To all the details of the event of creation – about the make-up of the spiritual realms of the finer-material universes and also the coarse-material universes – he gives detailed explanations in answer to Gabriele's questions.

Together with his dual, Gabriele, the Cherub of divine Wisdom, Brother Emanuel, is primarily responsible in the work of the Christ of God and leads it directly through her, the prophetess.

Gabriele speaks about all this with the greatest naturalness, without any fuss. Totally at ease, she speaks in normal everyday language, of the greatest event, the creation.

Of course, the terms are often lacking, because, as stated, in our three dimensionally-shaped world, there is no language for the seven-dimensional events. But her pictorial depiction allows us to intuit many a thing that goes far beyond all previous knowledge about the emergence of the All, the cosmos, about the event of creation and the continuing evolution of the infinite Being.

How Manuscripts Develop

Gabriele's creativity is inexhaustible. Particularly when it involves working for the Kingdom of God, she is a constant source of new ideas. There is always something new in the making.

When she writes a new book or a program manuscript, then everything comes together seamlessly. Her own written manuscripts develop in the shortest time – when not overlaid by other worries and needs of the work of the Christ of God. From her opened consciousness, out of which she draws, the words and sentences flow nearly print-ready and do not need any editing. But Gabriele herself often goes over her texts once more – and her ever-active spirit could compose, in turn, whole brochures and books from each sentence and each word. We are often privileged to experience how she breaks down and continues to unfold what is already given. She could come up with ever more facets, so that she often has to restrain herself from explaining everything that could still be given as a part of the content. And when we then find no more words, because we are fascinated by her explanations on the spiritual principles of life and the workings of the mighty Creator-Spirit, she calmly says: "And all that is trifling in relation to what unfolds in me and cannot be passed on in our words."

Manuscripts for many of the radio and television programs that Gabriele does not compose herself also develop based on her suggestions. And planned discussions for this are not even needed. On the contrary, during a meal together or during other incidents, often during a drive in the car, conversations develop during which whole manuscripts develop. Gabriele's brilliant formulations, her coined words and profound analyses constitute the spiritual relevance and significance of these conversations, which then are often worked into radio and television programs.

When a manuscript is being developed, she is inexhaustible with her esprit and her ideas, rich in content.

When two of us are sitting together to develop a new manuscript, Gabriele frequently telephones, asking: "Have you already included this?" and then suggests totally new thoughts, which are so evident and further our efforts, so that each time we are amazed anew.

The Designer

The nature of the divine Wisdom is the deed. Creative design is her element. Gabriele is the Seraph of divine Wisdom, and her inherent artistic, creative nature is always expressed in all that she does. Again and again, she surprises us with her ideas of design. Again and again, she challenges the experts to take unusual paths, to try out things that in her inner being she knows are possible. In this, too, she totally lives the words from the Lord's Prayer of Jesus of Nazareth: *on earth as it is in heaven"–* however, always transformed-down to the possibilities of the three dimensions.

Gabriele's warm-hearted, youthful nature, her motivating and always forward-striving manner fill others with enthusiasm. Her vitality and dynamism is infectious where putting new ideas into practice. In all the practical helpful tips she gives, according to the respective circumstances, she is totally committed and leaves nothing unheeded until a solution to the situation has been found and further steps are worked out and set in motion.

It is also her special skill to change and transform something already on hand, so that valuable new creations emerge.

Where professionals would often choose the way they learned, with modern techniques and corresponding styling, Gabriele amazes us again and again with ideas on how existing things, often even dilapidated buildings and spaces, can be made into picture-perfect gems.

She loves to furnish rooms beautifully.
In the process, she usually resorts to what is on hand and uses all the elements that are available without a lot of effort, in order to create, with relatively simple means, a thing of beauty that gives the spaces harmony and consonance.

Although in my profession I had a lot to do with creative people, I have never met anyone who, from within themselves, has developed such a gift for designs of beauty, so that for each room, for each building, for each garden, in one moment, there is a fullness of design ideas that invariably fit together into a harmonious whole.

Gabriele's amazing ingenuity also extends to fashion design. She has created many a model, which, one or two seasons later, we discovered with the big fashion designers. Hardly has Gabriele taken a piece of material in hand, but what she already has the fitting idea for what could be created from it.

Gabriele is also a very creative person in her own personal sphere; she is constantly changing and beautifying. A continual creative effect draws through her rooms, which are finely and nobly arranged according to their respective possibilities, with a clean, pure atmosphere that corresponds to her nature. Her absolute sense of beauty and her love for well cared-for things are also expressed in Gabriele's home, which she has furnished with style, charm and decided comfort. Her sense of beauty always lends the rooms a casual freshness; every item has its place and nothing useless lies around.

When she is occupied with new ideas for the elements of design, she has an incredibly captivating way of conveying these ideas to the artisans. It is not seldom that the latter frequently reach the limits of their expertise, so that they sometimes have to combine all their talents to master the challenge.

With a decidedly aesthetic sense, Gabriele combines a richness of ideas, oriented toward the practical and the solution.

We could experience how this is accomplished, when, from her abundance of ideas and without a lot of preliminary planning by architectural and engineering firms, within six weeks Gabriele converted a large, rectangular meeting hall into the *Sophia Library of the Free Spirit*. Together with a crew of enthusiastic artisans, this could be accomplished within such a short time, because Gabriele was at the building site daily giving suggestions and ideas for creative solutions. Visitors to the *Sophia Library* marvel again and again at the special atmosphere and the detailed beauty offered by the vibrantly blue room.

The Tent of God Among the People for All Nations of this Earth, Under the Sign of the Lily, the Ark of the Covenant of the Free Spirit – New Jerusalem is also based on ideas and design suggestions from Gabriele. Again and again, experts spend hours discussing architectural challenges, for which Gabriele finds an astoundingly ingenious solution within a few minutes.

When she is active in giving form to the Land of Peace as a landscape gardener, as it were, this also takes place in a fascinating way. First she expresses the idea that is in her inner being as a picture. An initial on-site inspection often brings up very specific ideas, from which further aspects gradually open up, usually within a few days. During the further progress of the construction and design measures, the respective factors are included and with a certainty of design, the most beautiful formations are produced in the midst of nature.

Often the first visit is a very simple one. On the great park-like grounds of the Land of Peace of the *International Gabriele Foundations*, Gabriele strode with large steps across the meadows and fields and scattered pebbles and stuck in wooden sticks to outline the approximate size of the final site.

At the site of the large Christ-Rock Fountain, first an enormous 60-ton granite boulder was "simply" placed in the midst of a meadow that Gabriele said would be a nice site. Soon afterward a large water basin was built around the rock. Already present material, such as a stone biotope, bushes and trees were integrated by Gabriele into the new, Mediterranean-style planting, which is surrounded by beds of white pebbles.

Today, the parklike area has become a real oasis of stillness, which attracts many people again and again, due to its unique radiation. Thus, the Land of Peace, on which Gabriele has created a blossoming habitat for nature and animals, offers peace-loving people a place of inner contemplation in the midst of nature's fullness of life.

Gabriele's Nature

How can one describe such a multifaceted being as Gabriele? Words always remain only inadequate descriptions that cannot do justice to her true nature.

But what I can say with certainty is the following:
Gabriele, whom I have experienced, and experience, as thoroughly natural, endearing and upright, is faithful to God, the Eternal, in all her work, and bows solely to His will.

She is kind and warm-hearted, where giving assistance to a fellow creature – be it a plant, an animal or a human being – is concerned. She is generous in her thoughts and works, modest in her demeanor, purposeful and clear regarding the fulfillment of the laws of God.

She endures much, but she does not tolerate the mockery of Christ, of God and of the Kingdom of God.

She is unceasingly creative.

Thanks to Gabriele, what the Christ of God in Jesus of Nazareth announced is being fulfilled: The Comforter is here; the Spirit of truth has led us into all the truth; His coming is prepared; the messianic and sophianic age has begun.

Gabriele – in her, the being of the divine Wisdom, Sophia – is the last link in the series of high spirit beings before God's throne that incarnated in a human body. Like a string of pearls, the incarnations of the law-pairs before the throne of God line up in the Redeemer-work of the Christ of God. The bow of light is drawn, from Abraham to Gabriele.

Gabriele works in God and God works through her.

The Divine Wisdom, Sophia, Who Prepares the Way for the Christ of God

"I know Gabriele" – a bold statement, when you know that the Seraph of divine Wisdom lives in Gabriele and works for the Kingdom of God in unceasing unity with the Cherub of divine Wisdom. In her sisterly fashion, every now and then and with simple words, Gabriele lets it be known that everything that she still knows and what she has endured for the Kingdom of God in the finer-material realm of the fight of the light against the darkness is merely a reflection of the dimension of her divine-spiritual work in unity with the Cherub of divine Wisdom. Thus, behind the dimensions visibly accessible to us, events of a cosmic magnitude are taking place, of which Gabriele only rarely speaks, because we human beings can hardly grasp them.

And yet, whether we human beings are able to grasp it or not: The regent-pair of the divine Wisdom presides over the work of redemption of the Christ of God, the Co-Regent of the Kingdom of God, and is responsible for leading home all souls and ensouled human beings – not only on the Earth and in the purification planes:

The work of the Christ of God encompasses the dimensions of all Being, from the level of Order up to the preparation levels of the eternal Being, so that the children of God may once again cross over the threshold of Mercy into the pure Being of the eternal creation of Being, into the Kingdom of God. To remedy, dissolve, transform and guide home everything that lies in-between, everything that is opposed to this, lies in the immeasurable divine mission of the divine Wisdom – Sophia.

As a woman in service of the Eternal, Gabriele faithfully and humbly bears the knowledge of this and the burden of this all-encompassing mission. Even though many people let themselves be fooled by Gabriele's modesty and simplicity, in all that she does she is indeed the exalted woman who prepares the way for the Christ of God.

I not only know this in my heart, it is also visible, because everything, absolutely everything, that was, and is, given through Gabriele, bears the fruits that are from God.

It is the being of the heavens, the Seraph of divine Wisdom, Sophia, that unceasingly works for the homeland in the human being, Gabriele.

May the one who can grasp it, grasp it; may the one who wants to leave it, leave it. But anyone who has a heart for Christ feels what a great event is taking place in our time.

Martin Kübli

Another Contemporary Witness

In the introduction to the previous chapter, it was explained why it is so difficult to convey a picture of Gabriele to our fellow people and to the people of future generations that even remotely does justice to her, the human being Gabriele, as well as the great prophetess and emissary of God in our time.

In any case, from my own perception, I can confirm what is reported in the previous chapter. When I was privileged to experience Gabriele for the first time about 30 years ago, I was deeply impressed by her grace and beauty, by her warmhearted and sensitive nature, by her strength and dynamism and by every word that she spoke out of herself, from her opened consciousness, or that the Kingdom of God revealed through her. Everything was consistent with one another; everything radiated a harmony and truthfulness as I had never before experienced. And at the same time, Gabriele conducted herself modestly and with reserve, but so friendly and accommodating, that you had the feeling of meeting a long-time friend or acquaintance. In over 30 years until this day, nothing has changed with this impression.

Again and again, Gabriele is an example and shining role model of the love for God and neighbor that is lived, for a life according to the commandments of the Kingdom of God, just as Christ taught and lived in Jesus of Nazareth 2000 years ago, and as He teaches again today in the Spirit, via the prophetic word through Gabriele.

With Gabriele, it is this self-evident unison of word and deed, of teaching and living, linked with Gabriele's impressive nature, which allows one to surmise what an extraordinary woman lives among us.

Many a one who is confronted for the first time with the question of whether a being from the Kingdom of God can be living among us as a prophetess, and who is not kept by religious blinders from approaching this question with reason and common sense, will examine the person of the prophet and what he speaks and does. If he does this conscientiously, he will conclude that each word from Gabriele, each expression of life, her entire behavior, her whole life is one single proof that a true prophetess and emissary of the Kingdom of God lives among us. Everything that has been given to us as elucidation, schooling and teaching from the Kingdom of God through her is completely in harmony with itself and with the divine teachings of the Christ of God, which He brought to us as Jesus of Nazareth.

And the fullness of the revelations and schoolings of the truth from the Kingdom of God have reached a magnitude that can only be described as gigantic. Much of this has already been extensively presented in previous chapters of this book. During the entire known history of humanity, with the exception of Jesus, the Christ of God, there has never been anyone who personified and brought to the Earth anything that is comparable or similar.

And yet, much of what lies in Gabriele, the Seraph of divine Wisdom, is not even generally known. Everything that Gabriele says and does, she does exclusively out of love for, and in honor of, God, the Eternal, in order to serve Him and Christ in leading home all the fallen children of God.
Of her own accord, she does not speak of anything that does not serve this goal.

From a human viewpoint, there would often be reason to publicly put right or explain things, for instance, when someone or other gives himself airs in the world with things, or with discoveries he thinks he has made in areas of which the true correlations are apparent to Gabriele in all details and as a matter of course.
But if it is not crucial for the well-being of people, of nature and the Mother Earth, there is no reason for the Kingdom of God and thus, also for Gabriele, to intervene in the world of human posing and displays of ego. God, the Free Spirit, is freedom, which He leaves to each person according to that person's will.

To be clear about what I'm referring to here, I would like to give just a few examples of the fields of knowledge, beyond every human conception, that have been opened up by Gabriele's consciousness, which is anchored in the Spirit of God:

Gabriele's consciousness is not only open for dialogues with the Kingdom of God, on Earth, too, it is not subject to the limits we know. Via her consciousness, Gabriele can establish communication with every natural organism. For Gabriele, it is a matter of course – and I have often experienced this – to communicate with plants and animals, not by way of an external language, but with her consciousness via the indwelling divine aspects of the collective or of the part-soul of the respective plant or animal.

By way of her consciousness, Gabriele could also establish communication with every soul no matter where it may be. In the same way, she could see through every person, no matter how much this person tries to disguise himself before her. However, she will not reveal what she perceives. The Spirit of God, who sees and knows all things, betrays no one, and Gabriele likewise keeps to this.

Another example is Gabriele's ability to spontaneously know, by way of her opened consciousness, the correct reaction in all situations. This is particularly evident where especially intellectual people, who cleave to the world and are shaped by class consciousness, consider themselves to be particularly great during appearances and speeches in public.

I have experienced Gabriele in hundreds of situations, in which she gave people a profound answer to every question in next to no time, and in which she, without any preparation, made fundamental and often groundbreaking explanations of any length on individual topics, which until today, and unchanged, are still distributed in books or radio and television programs.

Gabriele did not learn all this, let alone study it. It is the Spirit of God, the Free Spirit, which flows unhindered in and through her. Even though many may not grasp this, one group of people has indeed grasped it: the caste of priests, particularly the functionaries of the institutions that call themselves Christian. They were invited several times to speak in public with Gabriele about God. None of those who pride themselves on having studied God or pretend to be legitimate successors to the prophets or even representatives of Christ on Earth, have ever dared to publicly face the mighty Spirit of God in Gabriele. The priests of our time reacted just like their predecessors in the temple at Jerusalem who were not equal to the boy Jesus, namely, with perfidious defamation and persecution.

An especially impressive example of how limited worldly knowledge is compared to the divine Wisdom, which Gabriele personifies, is given by so-called science. Just think of the fuss that is made worldwide when, for instance, somewhere or other a "scientist" presents something new about the emergence of the world and the universe – which is then replaced several years later by new knowledge.

While the "wise" of this world grope around in the dark, the divine Wisdom that knows about all things, lives among us and is ignored by the intellectuals with their learned fragmentary knowledge. For nearly 40 years, the Kingdom of God has been giving explanation after explanation in the prophetic word through Gabriele, from the origin and make-up of the creation of Being to the emergence of our universe, our world and all life on Earth.

The administrators of worldly knowledge do not want to know anything about God, the Eternal, and His prophetess and emissary, nor about the eternal truth. That is why their knowledge is often merely opinion and speculation, hypotheses or theory based on false assumptions; in any case, it is always only a pale reflection of the eternal truth, which the Kingdom of God reveals to us through Gabriele.

All this and much more, the entire divine knowledge, exists in the plain and modest woman whom we may call

Gabriele. A look into one day in Gabriele's life may show how close the Kingdom of God is to Gabriele at every moment:

On this day, the Cherub of divine Wisdom, Gabriele's dual in the spirit, whom we know as Brother Emanuel, speaks in a small circle through Gabriele about the divine pre-creations. He explains again and again that one cannot comprehensively describe the gigantic event with the words of the three dimensional world. But I would like to pass on here what we learned through the small crack in the door that Brother Emanuel opened for us:

There were pre-creations, but I do not want to go into them here. Before the eternal creation of Being, there were four powers – human beings call them gods – one with them was the primordial God, to whom the four powers gave their ideal image, the Father-Mother-God, the three filiation attributes for the eternal Being.

The primordial birth of the Father-Mother-God was active in the four powers, also called gods. The three powers of Order, Will and Earnestness gave to the creating and drawing power of the Wisdom, a great part of their energies of Wisdom, so that the creating and drawing power, the Wisdom, increased mightily in energy, and thus, together with Order, Will and Earnestness, the primordial Being in the primordial God, Kindness, Love and Gentleness, came into being.

From this primordial Being, Order, Will, Wisdom, Earnestness, Kindness, Love and Gentleness, Love and Wisdom created, and create, because God is the primordial power of the Love. That is why we hear again and again: »Love and Wisdom«; this combination developed during the pre-creations.

And when we want to describe the spiritual atom – as Brother Emanuel explained to us with simple words *– then the primordial nucleus of the spiritual atoms is always the Love in unity with Kindness and Gentleness. The four powers of creation and drawing – Love and Wisdom in unity with Order, Will and Earnestness – revolve around the primordial nucleus of the spiritual atoms.*

Brother Emanuel explained all this in the small circle.

This brief look lets us intuit the dimensions in which the communication between Brother Emanuel and Gabriele takes place. The gate to the Kingdom of God stands wide open. Two beings – the prince-pair of the divine Wisdom from the Kingdom of God – are linked with one another. The Cherub, the law-angel before God's throne, works in the spirit together with Gabriele, the Seraph in the earthly garment.

Gabriele is a human being for this walk over the Earth, but her true origin is the Kingdom of God, her homeland and ours. In eternity she was, and is, the Seraph of divine Wisdom, for us human beings the exalted woman, the lily of God, Sophia. The last section of this book is dedicated to her.

Gert Hetzel

Gabriele,
the Exalted Woman,
the Lily of God,
Sophia

What is written in this book by Gabriele herself and by her companions about her life and working is surely apt to leave a deep impression on the reader. Anyone who reads with an open heart receives insights into an extraordinary life and into an extraordinary lifework of an extraordinary human being, a woman who, without any kind of pomp or personality cult, lives modestly and reserved among her fellow human beings. Anyone who concerns himself more closely with Gabriele, with her person and her lifework, will reach the conclusion that he is a contemporary witness to the positive life and working of a human being that is unique in the known history of humankind.

But can an appreciation of Gabriele amount to nothing more than this realization? She herself would never utter a word about who the great being truly is, whom we know as Gabriele, because everything that she does, she does solely out of love for, and in honor of, God, the All-Highest, and His Son, the Christ of God.

But when in His great revelation of August 14, 2016, which we reported about in the foreword of this book, God, the Eternal, Himself opened the eyes of mankind, as to who is living among us as a human being, then at the end of this book it stands to reason to span the bow from Gabriele's life and working among the people to her origin as the Seraph of divine Wisdom in the Kingdom of God, the Sophia, to whom the All-Highest presented the lily as a symbol of purity, love and wisdom. Moreover, in this divine revelation by the Eternal lies the indication of the future, the working of Sophia in the coming messianic and sophianic age.

It is apparent that merely by looking at the life and workings of the human being Gabriele, as impressive and unique as they are, the true nature and greatness of Gabriele does not open up, if we do not try to look beyond the limits of our three-dimensional world.

How much this realization applies to most people, we learn from Christ, the Son of God, in His great work of revelation *This Is My Word. Alpha and Omega. The Gospel of Jesus*, which was published in 1989.

In this fundamental work, the Christ of God speaks to the people of our time and of the time to come about His life as Jesus of Nazareth and about the events of our days, in which Gabriele lives among us as the prophetess and emissary of God. There, we read the following about Gabriele in our time:

The first pioneers for the New Era did not yet recognize the great light that lived among them, because the incarnated part-ray of divine Wisdom behaved as a sister among brothers and sisters, without distinguishing herself. This modest sisterliness, which sprang from great humility and reverence before God, then also brought about true brotherliness and sisterliness among some of the pioneers. For them, the high bearer of light was a sister who could advise them in every situation and circumstance of life, because her spiritual body was one with God, the life. (p. 287)

For more than 40 years now, Gabriele has been living and working among us as a sister, as the teaching prophetess and emissary of the Kingdom of God. Through the explanation from the Kingdom of God, we know about Gabriele's divine origin and that in her, the Seraph, the female part of the prince-pair of the divine Wisdom before God's throne, has come to the Earth. Her dual, the male part, the Cherub of divine Wisdom, is known to many of us as spiritual teacher Brother Emanuel, who, from the Kingdom of God, works in the spirit garment together with his dual in the earthly garment, Gabriele. And from the many teachings of the Spirit of the Christ of God, many of us know that in the work of the Christ of God, the Cherub of divine Wisdom, on behalf of the Almighty and of His Son, Christ, is the responsible being for leading home all ensouled human beings and also the souls in the realms of the beyond.

However, even though we know about Gabriele's divine origin, even though many of us have experienced, and experience, how Gabriele tirelessly puts her incomparable talents and abilities to use for the well-being of her neighbor and second neighbor, nature and the animals, it is evident that the fewest people are aware of who truly lives among us in the human being, the modest woman, Gabriele.

In another passage of His great work of revelation *This Is My Word. Alpha and Omega. The Gospel of Jesus*, Christ unmistakably expresses this:

... the exalted woman, too – the spirit being in the earthly garment who lives among them to prepare the way for Me, the Christ – is, as with me in Jesus of Nazareth, recognized by just a few people, but not by the world, nor by all those within the inner circle. (p. 920)

In the words of revelation by the Christ of God, how close the connection is between the life and work of Gabriele and the life and work of the Christ of God as Jesus of Nazareth, is indicated again and again. This is very clearly expressed in the following explanation:

... many people talked about the Messiah and did not recognize Me because I lived among the people as Jesus of Nazareth. Many people talk – as was conveyed a long time ago – about an exalted woman who precedes the Lord, to prepare the way for Him. She is among the people as a human being – yet they do not recognize her. Just as I went unrecognized from the Earth, she, too, will similarly leave the Earth unrecognized. Many will continue to wait for the exalted woman who prepares the way for Me, the Christ; and yet, she was already among them.

Only when the time is ripe, when the truth breaks through, will the people recognize that the part-ray of divine Wisdom in the earthly garment was among them: the exalted woman in Me, the Christ, and we in God, our eternal Father, for the New Era, the Kingdom of the Christ. (p. 921)

In the events of her life on Earth, as well, many parallels can be recognized, above all in the reactions of the caste of priests and the mighty of this world toward the highest being from the Kingdom of God.

The people at the time of Jesus of Nazareth were expecting a king, who should liberate them from the yoke of Roman occupation and establish an external kingdom. At that time, in an externalized and violent, sinful world, the kingdom of the inner being, the Kingdom of God, was not close to their heart. That is why it was possible for the priestmen of His time to subject Jesus to the infamous murder on the cross by the state.

It is similar again today. Anyone in our world who surrounds himself with pageantry and glamour and offers the greatest show is idolized. The basest instincts are served; violence and immorality celebrate triumph in the government, in society and with the administrators of religious concerns. Their leaders are admired, revered and often even idolized. And on the other hand, millions of people are dying of hunger, and the climate and the Earth and everything that grows and lives on it are being destroyed step by step. The Kingdom of God, the kingdom of the inner being, is farther than ever from most people, not least of all due to the centuries-long indoctrination by the demonic distortion of divine laws into the pagan rites and doctrines of cassock-wearers and their habits and behavior that are far from God.

And like Jesus, the Christ, 2000 years ago, Gabriele has also been exposed to a decades-long way of the cross consisting of infamous defamation, discrimination and persecution by the priestmen of our time.

An explanation can be found in this for the fact that the majority of people in our time cannot grasp, in turn, who lives among us in the messenger from the Kingdom of God, in the prophetess and emissary of God, Gabriele. But according to the words of the Christ of God, why does this also apply to the people who know that Gabriele is the Seraph of divine Wisdom, that in our time, together with the Cherub of divine Wisdom, the responsible servant in the work of the Lord, she leads the homebringing of all fallen beings to the Kingdom of God, of the heavenly Father of all His children – many of whom have themselves experienced Gabriele in many public events or know her from the hundreds of divine revelations that have come to the Earth through Gabriele, or from the thousands of pages written by her?

The Christ of God also answers this question in the Christ-revelation *This Is My Word. Alpha and Omega. The Gospel of Jesus*:

It is an old concept of man that each of his fellowmen should be just as he, himself, is. Thus, many people make differences only between outer wealth and poverty, but not between the inner wealth and poverty of the soul. They cannot recognize or distinguish inner processes. For this reason, they see every person from the perspective of their human ego. To them, their fellowman has only the significance which their ego attributes to him. This is why the messengers of God in the earthly garment are not recognized, and the words of life that flow through them are accepted by only a few as being the word of God, the law of life. (p. 197)

It is apparently very difficult for us to see beyond the edge of our egocentric consciousness that is limited by the three dimensions, anyway. As long as we try to fathom the nature and greatness of a divine being only from the perspective of our earthly existence, of our earthly horizon, without ourselves setting out on the path of purity and love, the messianic path in the sophianic age, which the Sophia in Gabriele has brought us, presumably little will change about this.

And yet the decisive event, the mighty revelation of God, the Eternal, from August 14, 2016, which is already given in the foreword of this book, encourages us to try to grasp the words of the Eternal, and, from this perspective, to look at the infinite dimensions of the Kingdom of God with new eyes, at the grandeur, the direct unity in God, the Eternal, the true origin of the great divine Seraph of Wisdom, the Sophia, who lives among us as a plain and simple woman, as Gabriele, the prophetess and emissary of God.

Let us turn once more to the message of the All-One. It is the highest power of love, God, the Eternal, who speaks to us, the Creator of all Being, of the entire universe, the All-Spirit, who manifested Himself in the highest being, whom we may call Father.

It is He, the Eternal All-One, who gives us an inkling of which place Gabriele, the part-ray of the divine Wisdom, occupies in the Kingdom of God as the daughter directly created by the Eternal Himself, when He says:

I, who I Am, present the lily to My daughter from My primordial heart, who has assumed the prophetic word for Me and is the emissary of the eternal kingdom.

As a human being, she is the expression of Sophia, the Wisdom, to whom I present the lily. My word, the truth, spoke, and speaks through her. My word of purity is the prophetic word and the voice of Wisdom.

I Am who I Am, from the primordial beginning. She is who she is, from Me, from the primordial beginning. Before the act of creation, she was in Me as My ideal image and will, and I created her as My image.

I sent My image, the primordial Wisdom, the divine Wisdom, to the human beings. She became a human being, was a human being and is still a human being among the human beings, My primordially eternal ideal image.

I was the word through her. I Am the word through her. In her soul, I Am the primordial Being, the lily, which she places into the hearts of all people who walk the path of purity and love, the messianic path in the sophianic age.

The esteem and the deep bond of the Eternal with His daughter, the Sophia, the divine Wisdom, which is expressed in these words, is overwhelming. Already before the first act of creation, before the All assumed form, Sophia was the ideal image and will of the divine primordial Being, of God, the Eternal, manifested as His image at the beginning of the creation event.

During the days following this revelation by the Eternal from the Kingdom of God, we received further impulses for a deeper understanding of the divine creation, of the creation of the divine Wisdom, of the Love and Wisdom of God. Thus, among other things, we learned from the Kingdom of God:

The divine Wisdom – two and yet one – are eternally linked in the unity before God's throne. God's creation, spiritually giving and spiritually receiving, is described by us human beings as male and female, or as positive and negative, Cherub and Seraph.
United, both powers form the Wisdom of God as a unit. Beheld and created for infinity by the Eternal – and the one part sent to the Earth to teach humankind: Sophia.

The Cherub of divine Wisdom, called Brother Emanuel by us human beings, was the teacher of Wisdom for Sophia, who followed the path of prophecy on behalf of the Almighty.

We learned more about the divine Wisdom and the mighty event of creation:

The first day of creation is the workpiece of God, the deed. He, the Eternal, beheld and created. From His heart's chamber, He beheld and created Wisdom, two poles merged into one pole, giving and receiving.

And He, the Eternal, looked into His primordial Being and saw in Himself His Son. He created Him out of Himself, His Mercy, His Love and Wisdom.

He beheld and created His seven primordial powers in the center of His Love, and He created.

He created His four powers of creation: Order, Will, Wisdom, Earnestness.

He beheld and created His three attributes: Kindness, Love and Gentleness, also called Patience, Love and Mercy.

He looked into His eternal Being and saw the gigantic primordial suns, to which He gave life and form through His four powers.

He beheld and created and His infinitely eternal Being, the Love, brought forth a people of children out of Kindness, Love and Gentleness.

He beheld and created and saw the unending planes, which He left to His four created powers, Order, Will, Wisdom and Earnestness, as His powers of shaping and creating.

He saw and it was good.

The seven powers of the Almighty, emerged from His primordial Being, are seven natures, giving and receiving in duality, called positive and negative – two and yet one.

That is the principle of the primordial creation of the eternal primordial Being, of the eternal primordial light, which we human beings also call the Primordial Central Sun.
Thus, it is understood that God, the loving and caring God-Father, will lead His children back through the Love in His Son and through the Love of Sophia, linked and seen as a unit: the Wisdom.
Therefore, the messianic and sophianic age.

Although we still cannot imagine the true dimension of the mighty event of creation and the part the divine Wisdom played in it, it becomes quite clear that there is nothing greater in all of the universe, and that Gabriele, who lives among us as a human being, is an essential part of this event.
Perhaps a comparison can also convey an inkling of what immense and incomprehensible dimensions and event we

are talking about here. Science assumes today that our material universe consists of approximately a thousand billion galaxies, each of which, in turn, consists of billions of stars – for instance, our Milky Way, of about one hundred billion stars.

From the Kingdom of God, we know that besides our material universe, there is still a much bigger part-material universe, and that both together, in turn, make up only a tiny fragment of the purely spiritual, divine universe.

All universes, all Being, all life – everything from the very beginnings and under the participation of the divine Wisdom, emerged from the primordial creation of the Father-Mother-God, from the primordial light, the Primordial Central Sun. And it is the part-ray of this divine Wisdom who lives among us in Gabriele and serves God, the Eternal, as prophetess and emissary. Transformed down to our profane level and spoken with our earthly words: The incarnated being in Gabriele was involved from the very beginnings of the Being!

This is why we hear over and over again about the Love and Wisdom that shaped and created. In the entire universe, the divine Wisdom, the deed, is the shaping, designing power. God's love is the highest force, the impulse-giver for the entire universe, for the entire creation, in the center of each spiritual atom, in all Being. And God's love is radiantly manifested in Christ, the first-beheld and first-created Son of God, the Co-Regent of the Kingdom of God, the bearer of the part-power from the primordial power.

And so, the Love and the Wisdom worked according to the will of the eternal All-One from the very beginning of the creation of the Being. And when several children of God turned against God and shadowed themselves ever more, so that they could no longer stay in the pure heavens of the Kingdom of God and finally took themselves into the depths along with several split-offs of spiritual planets, it was again the divine Love and Wisdom that went after all fallen beings and finally the human beings on matter, our Earth.

The greatest proof of this is the life and work of the Christ of God in Jesus of Nazareth. He, the Co-Regent of the Kingdom of God, took it upon Himself to go into the lower depths of the greatest shadowing and density on the Earth, to bring home to the eternal kingdom of His heavenly Father, all the children of God, which He had also accepted as His children. Many people say that Jesus of Nazareth redeemed humankind because He died on the cross. This explanation is a mockery of the Christ of God and of God-Father, which originates from the perfidy of the adversary of God, with which he wants to embellish the cowardly murder of the Son of the All-Highest through his vassals, and to make people forget the resurrection of the Christ of God, His victory over the adversary.

It is the "It is finished," with which Jesus, the Christ, redeemed the human beings.

Only in our time, does the scope of this event become evident again to humankind by way of Christ in the prophetic word through the divine Wisdom in Gabriele. From His part-power of the primordial power, He, the Christ of God, transferred His Redeemer-sparks to each soul and to each ensouled human being. It is His great deed as the Messiah, with which He ensured the return of all God's children to their eternal homeland, to the Kingdom of God.

The divine Wisdom also descended again and again into the lower depths of the Fall-realms and into our world, in order to rescue God's fallen children. Best known is the great prophet of God, Isaiah, who about 750 years before Christ foretold His appearance as the Messiah and a coming Kingdom of Peace. In Isaiah, the mighty law-angel before God's throne, the Cherub of divine Wisdom, was among the human beings.

Isaiah called upon the people of his time to desist from their godless doings and to turn to a life according to the laws of God.

From other prophets of the Old Covenant, we also know of their origin in the Kingdom of God from the divine Wisdom.

Again and again, in the traditional scriptures is indicated the workings of the divine Wisdom on Earth, which announced the appearance in the flesh on Earth of God's love in His Son, Christ, just as in our time, the divine Wisdom in Gabriele announces the appearance of the Christ of God on Earth in the spirit.

The collaboration of the divine Love and the divine Wisdom was explained to us in our time by the Cherub of divine Wisdom, who is familiar to us as the spiritual teacher, Brother Emanuel, with the following words:

At the behest of the Almighty and of His Son, I am the third basic power of God and the responsible one in the work of the Christ of God in leading home the ensouled children of God, the human beings and the souls in the spheres of the beyond.

Because the people 2000 years ago were not willing to follow the words of Jesus of Nazareth, the Christ of God – *Follow Me* – and instead handed Him over to the caste of priests and their accomplices in murder, Jesus, the Christ, the Son of God, announced 2000 years ago the Comforter, who would lead the people into all the truth.

This Comforter has come in our time. The Love, Christ, the Son of God, gives revelations through the divine Wisdom, through the prophetess and emissary of God, Gabriele. The divine Love and the divine Wisdom are working together again, so that today the whole truth from the Kingdom of God, insofar as it can be passed on in human words, is revealed in all its facets.

As already at the beginning of all Being, it is the divine Love and the divine Wisdom who are working together. In our time, they are leading the way, in order to lead all fallen beings, the entire Fall, back into the eternal homeland, in the messianic and sophianic age that God, the Eternal, has now announced.

The great cosmic being, the part-ray of the divine Wisdom, the Seraph of the prince-pair before God's throne, the ideal image, the image of God, the daughter of the infinitely eternal Father from His primordial heart – all this is Gabriele, who lives among us as a human being, as a sister.

Gabriele does not speak about this of her own accord; her modesty, her humility and reverence before God are too great. But for each one of us, for each reader of this book, the comprehension of Gabriele's origin and true nature can be an inestimable help, to perhaps be able to sense the cosmic context of all that Gabriele has given us under the simple statement:

A Woman's Life in Service of the Eternal

Suggested Reading

This Is My Word
A and Ω

The Gospel of Jesus

The Christ-Revelation which true Christians the world over have come to know

An encompassing Christ-Revelation given through the teaching prophetess and emissary of God, Gabriele. A book that allows you to know more about Jesus, the Christ. It is the truth about His workings and life as Jesus of Nazareth.

From the contents: Childhood and youth of Jesus • The falsification of the teaching of Jesus of Nazareth over the past 2000 years • Purpose and meaning of life on Earth • Jesus taught the law of cause and effect • Prerequisites for the healing of the body • Jesus taught about marriage • God does not rage and punish • The teaching of "eternal damnation" is a mockery of God • Jesus exposed scribes and Pharisees as hypocrites • Jesus loved the animals and always spoke up for them • About death, reincarnation and life • The true meaning of the Redeemer Deed of Christ ... and much, much more...

With a short autobiography of Gabriele

1078 pp., softbd, Order No. S007en
ISBN: 978-1-890841-38-6. 15.00 Euro

The Speaking All-Unity

The Word of the Universal Creator-Spirit

A Cosmic Work of Teaching and Learning from the School of Divine Wisdom

Taken from conversations with Gabriele
and compiled by
Martin Kübli and Ulrich Seifert

From the Big Bang to the question of why addictions, murder and natural disasters exist, you will find answers in this book to questions, which the denominational teachings leave unanswered. Learn about why it is so important for us to have a respectful and loving relationship with other living beings and what we can learn from the animals. Read about how you can find your way to a positive and fulfilled life, and finally to the All-Unity of the life.

From the contents: The make-up of the core of being in the Eternal's cradle of drawing and creating • The workings of the four primordial powers in the condensed Being • The Big Bang. What was before the Big Bang? • Our life film. We human beings live in pictures • Our primary warfare agents, the thoughts • Why the weapons arsenals of this world? • All living beings and life forms from God's creation are beings of the All-Unity – What separates us from the All-Unity, the communication with the eternal Creator-God? • We learn on ourselves • and much more.

Includes an Audio-CD with two meditations:
1. "Everything Is in Bloom" – a meditative virtual walk
2. "Our True Being" – a meditative cosmic view

382 pp., hardbd., many fotos, Order No. S173en
ISBN:978-1-890841-33-1, 29.00 Euro

We will be happy
to send you our free catalog

Gabriele Publishing House – The Word
Max-Braun-Str. 2,
97828 Marktheidenfeld, Germany

www.gabriele-publishing-house.com